Apress Pocket Guides

Apress Pocket Guides present concise summaries of cutting-edge developments and working practices throughout the tech industry. Shorter in length, books in this series aims to deliver quick-to-read guides that are easy to absorb, perfect for the time-poor professional.

This series covers the full spectrum of topics relevant to the modern industry, from security, AI, machine learning, cloud computing, web development, product design, to programming techniques and business topics too.

Typical topics might include:

- A concise guide to a particular topic, method, function or framework

- Professional best practices and industry trends

- A snapshot of a hot or emerging topic

- Industry case studies

- Concise presentations of core concepts suited for students and those interested in entering the tech industry

- Short reference guides outlining 'need-to-know' concepts and practices.

More information about this series at `https://link.springer.com/bookseries/17385`.

Securing Smart Things

A Hands-On Guide to Safeguarding Smart Systems

Massimo Nardone

Apress®

Securing Smart Things: A Hands-On Guide to Safeguarding Smart Systems

Massimo Nardone
HELSINKI, Finland

ISBN-13 (pbk): 979-8-8688-2366-4   ISBN-13 (electronic): 979-8-8688-2367-1
https://doi.org/10.1007/979-8-8688-2367-1

Managing Director, Apress Media LLC: Welmoed Spahr
Acquisitions Editor: Spandana Chatterjee
Editorial Assistant: Gryffin Winkler

Cover designed by eStudioCalamar

Distributed to the book trade worldwide by Springer Science+Business Media New York, 1 New York Plaza, New York, NY 10004. Phone 1-800-SPRINGER, fax (201) 348-4505, e-mail orders-ny@ springer-sbm.com, or visit www.springeronline.com. Apress Media, LLC is a Delaware LLC and the sole member (owner) is Springer Science + Business Media Finance Inc (SSBM Finance Inc). SSBM Finance Inc is a **Delaware** corporation.

For information on translations, please e-mail booktranslations@springernature.com; for reprint, paperback, or audio rights, please e-mail bookpermissions@springernature.com.

Apress titles may be purchased in bulk for academic, corporate, or promotional use. eBook versions and licenses are also available for most titles. For more information, reference our Print and eBook Bulk Sales web page at http://www.apress.com/bulk-sales.

Any source code or other supplementary material referenced by the author in this book is available to readers on GitHub. For more detailed information, please visit https://www.apress. com/gp/services/source-code.

If disposing of this product, please recycle the paper

I would like to dedicate this book to my children Luna, Leo, and Neve. Your love and support mean everything to me.

—Massimo

Table of Contents

About the Author

Massimo Nardone has more than 30 years of experience in information and cybersecurity for IT/OT/IoT/IIoT, web/mobile development, cloud, and IT architecture. His true IT passions are security and Android. He holds an M.Sc. degree in computing science from the University of Salerno, Italy.

Throughout his working career, he has held various positions starting as programming developer, then security teacher, PCI QSA, Auditor, Assessor, Lead IT/OT/SCADA/Cloud Architect, CISO, BISO, Executive, Program Director, OT/IoT/IIoT Security Competence Leader, etc. In his last working engagement, he worked as a seasoned Cyber and Information Security Executive, CISO, and OT, IoT, and IIoT Security Competence Leader helping many clients to develop and implement Cyber, Information, OT, and IoT Security activities.

He is currently working as Vice President of OT Security for SSH Communications Security.

He is an author of numerous Apress books, including *IAM and PAM Cybersecurity*, *Cybersecurity Threats and Attacks in the Gaming Industry*, *Industrial Control System (ICS) and Operational Technology (OT) Security*, *Secure RESTful APIs: Simple Solutions for Beginners*, and *Spring Security 6 Recipes*, and co-authored *Pro Spring Security, Pro JPA 2 in Java EE 8*, and *Pro Android Games. He has* reviewed more than 100 Apress titles.

About the Technical Reviewer

Mario Faliero is a telecommunications engineer and entrepreneur. He has more than 19 years' experience with radio 1 frequency hardware engineering. Mario has extensive experience in numerical coding, using scripting languages (MATLAB, Python) and compiled languages (C/C++, Java). He has been responsible for the development of electromagnetic assessment tools for space and commercial applications. Mario received his master's degree from the University of Siena.

Acknowledgments

Many thanks go to my wonderful children Luna, Leo, and Neve for supporting me all the time. You are and will be always the most beautiful reason of my life.

I want to thank my beloved parents Maria Ciniglio and Giuseppe Nardone, who always supported me and loved me so much. I will love and miss you forever.

Thanks to my beloved brothers, Roberto and Mario, for your endless love and for being the best brothers in the world.

Many thanks to Susan McDermott at Apress for giving me the opportunity to work as writer on this book.

—Massimo

CHAPTER 1

Foundations of IoT and the Security Landscape Description

The foundations of the Internet of Things (IoT) and the associated security landscape form a critical area of study and development in today's interconnected world. IoT refers to the vast and growing network of physical devices, sensors, actuators, embedded systems, and smart objects that communicate and share data over the internet. These devices range from everyday consumer products like smart thermostats and wearable health monitors to complex industrial systems, smart cities, and critical infrastructure. The core idea of IoT is to enhance automation, improve operational efficiency, and enable real-time decision-making by collecting, analyzing, and acting on data generated by these interconnected devices.

The foundational elements of IoT encompass a wide array of technologies, including wireless communication protocols, data analytics, cloud computing, embedded systems, and artificial intelligence. Together, they create a backbone that supports innovative applications across healthcare, manufacturing, transportation, agriculture, energy, and urban

© Massimo Nardone 2026
M. Nardone, *Securing Smart Things*, Apress Pocket Guides,
https://doi.org/10.1007/979-8-8688-2367-1_1

development. The benefits of IoT are substantial: improved quality of life, increased efficiency, cost savings, and enhanced safety. For example, in healthcare, IoT devices enable remote patient monitoring; in agriculture, they facilitate precise resource management; in smart cities, they optimize traffic flow and energy consumption.

However, as IoT expands its footprint, it also introduces significant challenges, particularly in the security domain. The interconnected nature of IoT devices increases the attack surface for cyber threats, with vulnerabilities stemming from device heterogeneity, limited computational resources, inconsistent security standards, and often inadequate updates or patching mechanisms. Malicious actors can exploit these vulnerabilities to launch attacks such as data breaches, device hijacking, or disruption of critical services, which could have severe consequences for safety, privacy, and operational continuity.

The security landscape of IoT is complex and constantly evolving. It requires a multilayered approach that encompasses device authentication, secure communication protocols, robust encryption, device integrity checks, and continuous monitoring for anomalies. Establishing trust between devices, ensuring data privacy, and safeguarding information during transmission and storage are essential components of a resilient IoT ecosystem. Moreover, regulations and standards are evolving to address these challenges, promoting best practices for security and privacy.

Addressing the security challenges of IoT also involves tackling issues related to scalability, device life cycle management, and interoperability. The sheer volume of devices and the diversity of technologies involved make unified security solutions difficult but essential. Developing security-by-design, embedding security features into devices from the outset, and fostering collaboration among stakeholders across industries are crucial steps toward building a safer IoT environment.

As IoT continues to evolve, the importance of understanding its foundational principles and the security landscape becomes paramount. Ensuring that IoT deployments are resilient, trustworthy, and privacy-preserving is essential to harness the full potential of this transformative technology. The future of IoT relies on advancing security measures alongside innovation, ensuring that the benefits of a connected world can be realized without compromising safety, privacy, or trust.

This new pocketbook delves into how the Internet of Things (IoT) is rapidly transforming industries, homes, and critical infrastructure by connecting billions of devices worldwide introducing however significant security risks.

In this chapter, we will start by providing an overview of IoT, including its architecture and ecosystems. It covers the types of IoT devices and applications, explains why IoT security matters, and highlights the most unique challenges.

Introduction and Definitions

First, let's introduce the major technologies and some of the differences.

- **Information technology (IT)** is the use of computers to store, retrieve, transmit, and manipulate data, or information, often in the context of a business or other enterprise.

- **Consumer technology (CT)** is hardware and software utilized by the end user (e.g., homes, phone apps, etc.).

- **Operational technology (OT)** is hardware and software that detects or causes a change through the direct monitoring and/or control of physical devices such as valves, pumps, temperature sensors, gas sensors, etc., within industrial processes.

- **The Internet of Things (IoT)** is the network of physical devices, vehicles, appliances, and other items embedded with electronics, software, sensors, actuators, and connectivity which enables these things to connect and exchange data.

- **Industrial IoT (IIoT)** is a subset of IoT.

  IIoT are IoT systems that connects and integrates industrial control systems with enterprise systems, business processes and analytics. (Industrial Internet Consortium Definition)

The technologies and how they interlink to each other are shown in Figure 1-1.

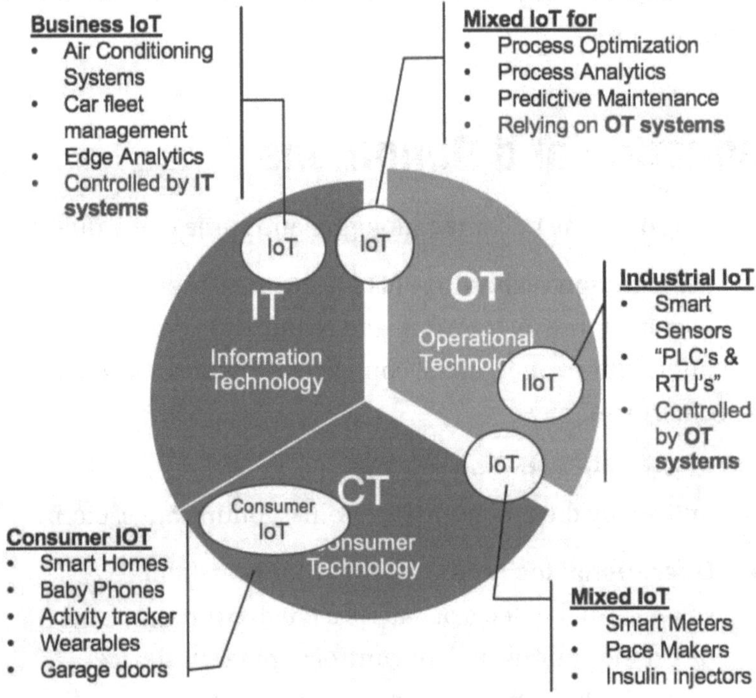

Figure 1-1. *The technologies' introduction*

Introduction of IoT and Differences with OT

The **Internet of Things (IoT)** refers to the network of **physical objects ("things")** that are embedded with **sensors, software, and connectivity** to collect and exchange data over the Internet.

These "things" can include everyday objects like home appliances, vehicles, wearables, machines, and industrial tools—basically, anything that can be connected to the internet and communicate without human intervention.

Operational technology (OT) refers to hardware and software that detects or causes changes through direct monitoring and control of physical devices, processes, and events within an enterprise.

Historically, OT systems were isolated and designed with minimal concern for cyber threats. However, the increasing integration of OT with IT networks, the advent of IoT (Internet of Things), and the rising sophistication of cyber threats have shifted the landscape dramatically. Today, safeguarding these systems requires new strategies and solutions tailored to their unique vulnerabilities.

Unlike IT, where the primary goals are confidentiality and accessibility, OT security emphasizes safety and reliability. Implementing effective OT cybersecurity involves using specialized software to monitor, analyze, and manage industrial systems and machinery, whether on-site or remotely. This software enables centralized access to all operational hardware, giving OT teams a comprehensive, real-time view of their entire infrastructure—from the endpoint devices to the control systems. Such visibility allows for rapid detection and resolution of anomalies, ideally before they cause significant damage or downtime.

OT security has become a critical necessity, particularly with the rise of the Internet of Things (IoT). IoT facilitates seamless communication between devices, delivering the convenience and efficiency demanded by modern households and businesses alike. Many warehouses and manufacturing plants have upgraded their equipment with interoperable, internet-connected capabilities to optimize operations—reducing the need for constant human oversight.

However, technological progress often introduces new vulnerabilities. As industrial systems adopt IoT, they inherit the cybersecurity risks associated with internet-connected devices.

Traditional IT cybersecurity solutions, designed primarily for data confidentiality and user access, are often insufficient for protecting OT interfaces and systems, which require tailored security measures to address their unique operational demands.

IoT Key Components

An IoT system connects the physical world with the digital world.

It typically consists of **five main components** working together to collect, transmit, analyze, and act on data:

- **Sensors/devices**
- **Connectivity/network**
- **IoT gateway/edge computing**
- **Cloud platform/data processing**
- **User interface/application**

Let's analyze a bit these five main IoT components.

Sensors, Devices, and Actuators

These are the "**things**" in the Internet of Things—physical objects equipped with sensors or actuators that gather data from the environment.

- **IoT Devices:** Physical objects equipped with sensors, actuators, processors, and communication interfaces that collect data and perform actions. They can include smart appliances, wearables, industrial equipment, or environmental monitors, enabling automation and remote management.

- **IoT devices** are equipped with sensors, communication modules, and actuators, enabling them to interact intelligently with the environment and other systems. They are used in smart homes, autonomous vehicles, industrial automation, healthcare, agriculture, and many other fields.

Components of IoT Devices:

1. **Sensors:** Detect environmental or physical parameters (temperature, humidity, motion, light, gases, etc.)

2. **Actuators:** Perform actions based on data or commands (motors, valves, fans, switches)

3. **Processor/Controller:** Processes sensor data and runs embedded software to make decisions

4. **Communication Module:** Connects the device to the cloud, local network, or other devices via Wi-Fi, Zigbee, Z-Wave, LTE-M, LoRA, or other protocols

5. **Power Supply:** Batteries, solar, or mains power source

Functionality of IoT Devices include

- **Data Collection:** Sensors gather data from their environment.

- **Data Transmission:** Collected data is sent to cloud platforms or local servers for analysis.

- **Processing and Analysis:** Cloud or edge computing algorithms analyze data to detect patterns or anomalies.

- **Action and Control:** Based on insights, devices or systems activate actuators or send notifications to optimize operations or enhance safety.

The IoT device diagram with components is shown in Figure 1-2.

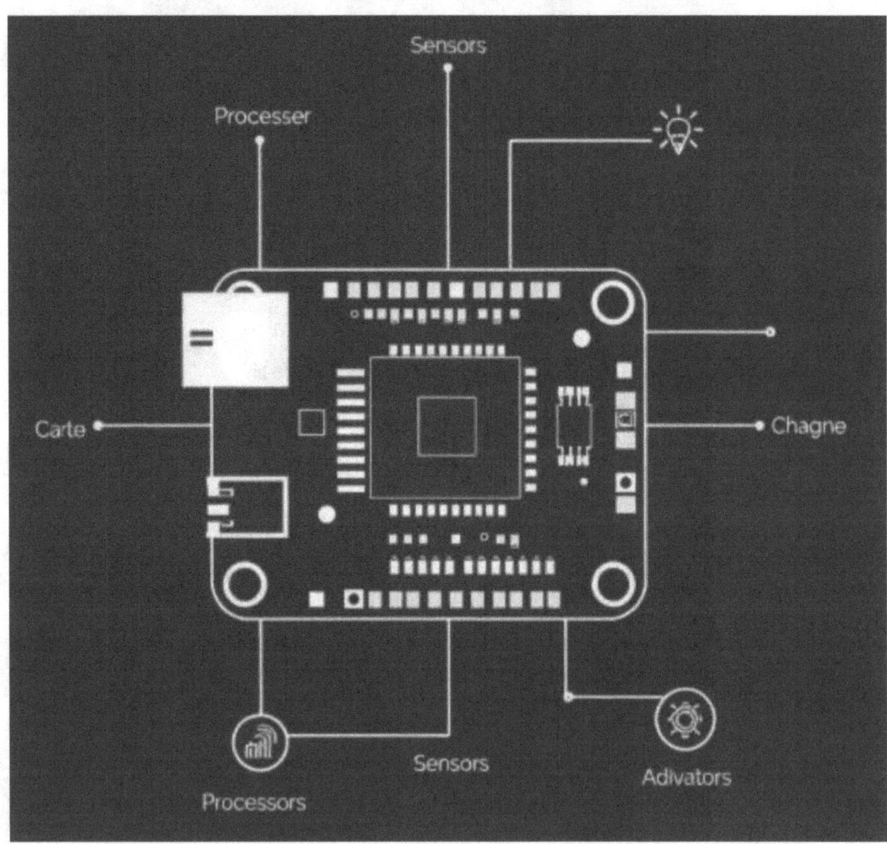

Figure 1-2. *The IoT device diagram with components*

Let's understand more the IoT sensors and actuators.

- **IoT Sensors:** Devices that detect and measure physical or environmental parameters such as temperature, humidity, pressure, motion, light, or gas levels. They convert these physical signals into electronic data that can be processed, stored, or transmitted within an IoT system.

- **IoT Actuators:** Devices that execute physical actions based on received data or commands, such as motors, valves, fans, or robotic arms. They alter the physical environment by turning electronic signals into mechanical movements or adjustments.

IoT Sensors

Sensors are essential for IoT, measuring physical changes—temperature, pressure, light, humidity—to transmit digital signals for processing by software.

The most common types of IoT sensors are listed here:

- **Motion Sensors:** Detect movement

- **Environmental Sensors:** Measure ambient conditions like temperature

- **Analog-to-Digital Converters:** Convert continuous values into data streams

- **Gas Sensors:** Detect gases and monitor air quality

- **Proximity Sensors:** Use infrared to trigger alarms based on object distance

IoT devices, the latest trend, comprise sensors, processors, and communication tools, enabling smart systems that automate workflows and manage functions like setting routines and alerts.

IoT sensors are generally classified as follows:

1. **Active vs. Passive:** Active require power; passive don't.

2. **Contact vs. Noncontact:** Contact sensors need physical contact; noncontact don't.

3. **Absolute vs. Relative:** Absolute give direct readings; relative compare to a baseline.

4. **Analog vs. Digital:** Analog provide continuous signals; digital convert data to binary.

5. **Miscellaneous Sensors:** Include chemical, biological, and other sensors.

IoT sensor types include temperature, proximity, pressure, humidity, optical, and gyroscope sensors, playing pivotal roles in diverse applications like automation, safety, and efficiency.

Sensors can be static or dynamic.

- **Static:** Includes accuracy, range, and sensitivity

- **Dynamic:** Covers response to changes over time, like zero-order systems' immediate response and first-order systems' gradual adjustment

Understanding these characteristics helps optimize sensor performance and select suitable sensors for specific IoT applications.

Examples:

- Temperature sensors in smart thermostats

- Motion detectors in security systems

- Industrial pressure sensors in IIoT systems

Some examples of IoT temperature sensors are shown in Figure 1-3.

Figure 1-3. *Examples of IoT temperature sensors*

IoT Actuators

IoT actuators are physical devices that receive commands from an IoT system to perform specific actions, thereby interacting directly with the environment. They transform electrical signals into mechanical movement or adjustment, enabling automation and control in smart environments.

The role of IoT actuators includes

- **Execute commands** based on data analysis or user input

- **Automate physical processes** such as opening a valve, turning on a motor, or adjusting a blind

- **Enhance system responsiveness** and enable real-time interaction between digital systems and the physical world

Some examples of IoT actuators are shown in Table 1-1.

Table 1-1. *Examples of IoT Actuators*

Type of actuator	Function/Use case	Example
Motors	Drive mechanical movement, such as opening/closing doors	Automated door openers
Valves	Control fluid flow in pipelines or tanks	Smart water/gas valves
Fans/pumps	Regulate air or liquid flow for climate or process control	HVAC systems, industrial pumps
Servos	Precise position control for robotics or cameras	Robotic arms, surveillance cameras
Relays	Switch electrical devices on/off	Lighting, appliances control

IoT actuators are crucial for creating **automated, intelligent environments**—from smart homes and buildings to industrial automation and autonomous vehicles—by translating digital commands into physical actions.

Some examples of IoT actuators are shown in Figure 1-4.

Figure 1-4. *Examples of IoT actuators*

Connectivity (Network Layer)

The data collected by sensors must be **transmitted** to other devices or the cloud.

Connectivity is what links IoT devices together and to processing systems.

- **Communication Technologies:** Wi-Fi, Bluetooth, Zigbee, LoRaWAN, NB-IoT, 5G, Ethernet, satellite, etc.

- Choice of network depends on **range, power, bandwidth, and cost** requirements

Example:

A smart irrigation system sending soil moisture data via LoRaWAN to a central gateway.

IoT Gateway/Edge Computing

IoT gateways act as intermediaries between devices and the cloud.

They collect, filter, and process data **closer to the source** before sending it onward—reducing latency and bandwidth use.

- Perform **local analytics** and **protocol translation**

- Enhance **security** by controlling data flow and authentication

Example:

An industrial edge gateway aggregates sensor data from a production line before transmitting summaries to the cloud.

Cloud/Data Processing Platform

This is the **brain of the IoT system** where large-scale data storage and analysis happen.

- Stores, manages, and analyzes data from millions of devices

- Uses **AI/ML algorithms** to detect patterns, optimize operations, or predict maintenance

- Can send control commands back to devices (closed-loop systems)

Examples:

AWS IoT Core, Microsoft Azure IoT Hub, Google Cloud IoT, and IBM Watson IoT

User Interface (UI)/Application Layer

The **front end** that allows users to interact with the IoT system—view data, configure devices, or take actions.

- Web dashboards, mobile apps, or control panels

- Often integrates with analytics and visualization tools

Examples:

- A smartphone app that controls home lighting or monitors energy consumption

- A web dashboard showing machine performance in a smart factory

IoT key components conceptual diagram is shown in Figure 1-5.

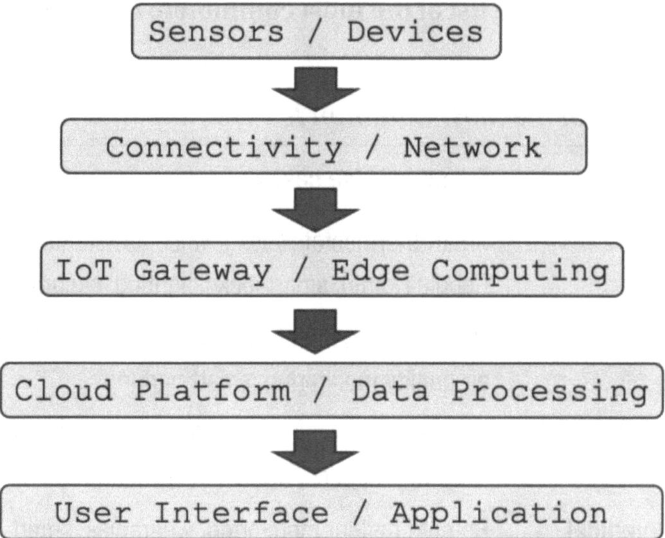

Figure 1-5. *IoT key components conceptual diagram*

Some elements cut across all layers of IoT architecture including

- **Security:** Encryption, authentication, access control, and secure firmware

- **Data Management:** Storage, standardization, and governance

- **Scalability:** Ability to support millions of devices

- **Integration:** APIs and interoperability among platforms and devices

In this book, we will mainly concentrate on the security element of IoT.

IoT Landscapes

Let's introduce now the typical IoT landscapes and then focus more on the security.

Table 1-2 shows the list of the most common IoT domain and industries.

Table 1-2. *List of the Most Common IoT Domain and Industries*

Domain	Examples/Use cases
Smart home	Smart thermostats (Nest), voice assistants (Alexa, Google Home), smart locks, lighting, security cameras
Smart city	Traffic management, waste collection, public lighting, air quality monitoring, smart parking
Industrial IoT (IIoT)	Predictive maintenance, industrial automation, asset tracking, robotics, SCADA integration
Healthcare/medical IoT (IoMT)	Remote patient monitoring, wearables, smart implants, connected medical devices
Agriculture (AgriTech/ smart farming)	Soil sensors, irrigation systems, livestock monitoring, drone-based crop analysis
Transportation/ automotive	Connected vehicles (V2X), fleet management, predictive maintenance, logistics tracking
Retail	Smart shelves, inventory tracking, customer analytics, connected vending machines
Energy/utilities	Smart grids, smart meters, renewable energy monitoring, oil and gas asset control
Building management/ smart infrastructure	HVAC systems, access control, occupancy sensors, energy efficiency management
Environmental monitoring	Weather stations, water quality sensors, pollution tracking, wildfire detection

Figure 1-6 shows some of the most typical IoT landscapes.

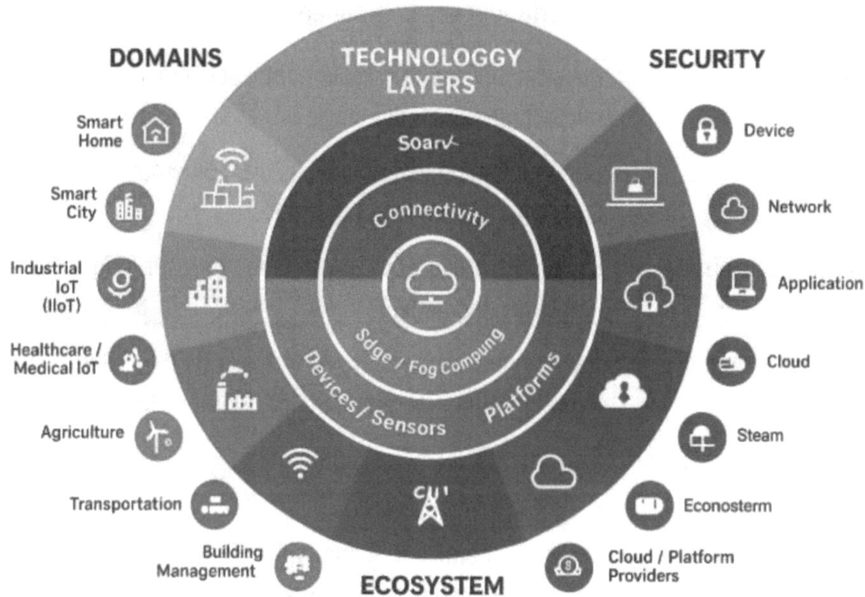

Figure 1-6. *IoT typical landscapes*

Then we must understand the IoT landscape by technology layer as shown in Table 1-3.

Table 1-3. *IoT Landscape by Technology Layer*

Layer	Description/Key components
Devices/sensors	Physical devices that collect data: sensors, actuators, microcontrollers, edge devices
Connectivity	Communication technologies: Wi-Fi, Bluetooth, Zigbee, LoRaWAN, NB-IoT, 5G, Ethernet
Edge/fog computing	Local data processing before cloud transfer (edge gateways, fog nodes)
Cloud platforms	Data storage, analytics, and orchestration (AWS IoT, Azure IoT Hub, Google Cloud IoT, Siemens MindSphere)
Applications/services	Dashboards, analytics, automation, AI/ML insights, mobile apps
Security layer	Device authentication, encryption, identity management, anomaly detection, PAM, Zero Trust
Data management/ analytics	Data pipelines, stream processing, predictive maintenance, machine learning models
Integration/APIs	Middleware and APIs connecting IoT devices to enterprise systems (ERP, MES, CRM)

IoT ecosystem players are shown in Table 1-4.

Table 1-4. *IoT Common Ecosystem Players*

Category	Examples
Hardware and devices	Intel, ARM, Raspberry Pi, Bosch, Siemens, STMicroelectronics
Connectivity providers	Cisco, Ericsson, Huawei, Nokia, Vodafone, AT&T
Cloud/platform providers	AWS IoT, Microsoft Azure IoT, Google Cloud IoT, IBM Watson IoT
Security vendors	Claroty, Palo Alto Networks, Fortinet, Armis, Nozomi Networks, Forescout
Industrial platforms (IIoT)	Siemens MindSphere, PTC ThingWorx, GE Predix, Schneider EcoStruxure
Standard bodies and alliances	IEEE, IETF, ISA, IEC, Industrial Internet Consortium (IIC), oneM2M, 3GPP

IoT Architectural Landscape

The architecture landscape of IoT describes the structured layers and components that enable the collection, processing, and action of data across interconnected devices. A well-designed architecture ensures secure, scalable, and efficient deployment of IoT solutions.

Core layers of IoT architecture include

1. **Perception layer (device layer)**

   - **Components:** Sensors, actuators, and embedded systems

   - **Function:** Collect environmental or physical data (temperature, humidity, motion, etc.) and perform initial processing or actuation

- **Example:** Temperature sensors in a manufacturing plant

2. **Network layer**

    - **Components:** Communication protocols (Wi-Fi, Zigbee, NB-IoT, LoRaWAN, LTE, 5G)

    - **Function:** Transmit data collected from perception devices to processing systems securely and reliably

    - **Example:** IoT gateways transmitting data to cloud servers

3. **Data processing layer**

    - **Components:** Edge computing devices, gateways, and fog nodes

    - **Function:** Filter, aggregate, and preprocess data locally to reduce latency and bandwidth use before sending it to cloud/data centers

    - **Example:** Local controllers analyzing machine vibrations

4. **Application layer**

    - **Components:** Cloud platforms, dashboards, analytics, and AI/ML algorithms

    - **Function:** Store, analyze, and visualize data; generate insights; support decision-making

    - **Example:** Real-time factory production dashboards

5. **Business layer**

- **Components:** Enterprise systems like ERP, maintenance management, and reporting

- **Function:** Use insights for operational decisions, predictive maintenance, and optimized workflows

- **Example:** Automated reorder systems or maintenance scheduling based on sensor data

Optional verticals include

- **Security Layer:** Integrated across all layers, encompassing encryption, authentication, and security policies

- **Integration Layer:** Combine IoT with existing enterprise systems and other data sources

The **IoT architecture landscape** is a multilayer ecosystem that spans device sensing, communication, data processing, and business decision-making. Proper design and security across these layers are essential for effective, reliable, and secure IoT deployment in environments like manufacturing, healthcare, smart cities, and more.

IoT Security Landscape

Let's introduce now the IoT security landscape.

The rapidly growing deployment of IoT devices across industries introduces significant security challenges and opportunities. The IoT security landscape encompasses a wide range of concerns, strategies, and technologies aimed at protecting IoT environments from threats, ensuring data integrity, privacy, and operational continuity.

Key components of IoT security landscape:

1. **Device security**

   - **Threats:** Unauthorized access, device tampering, and firmware attacks

   - **Mitigations**

     - Secure boot processes

     - Strong device authentication

     - Regular firmware updates

     - Hardware-based security features like Trusted Platform Modules (TPMs)

2. **Network security**

   - **Threats:** Eavesdropping, man-in-the-middle attacks, and unauthorized access

   - **Mitigations**

     - End-to-end encryption (TLS, DTLS)

     - Secure network protocols (Zigbee, Z-Wave, MQTT over TLS)

     - Network segmentation and firewall policies

     - VPNs and secure gateways

3. **Data security and privacy**

   - **Threats:** Data breaches, leaks, and unauthorized access

   - **Mitigations**

     - Data encryption both in transit and at rest

- Fine-grained access controls and role-based permissions

- Privacy policies complying with regulations like GDPR

4. **Cloud and back-end security**

   - **Threats:** Cloud account breaches and API vulnerabilities

   - **Mitigations**

     - Secure API gateways

     - Multifactor authentication (MFA)

     - Regular security assessments and patching

     - Monitoring and anomaly detection

5. **Identity and access management**

   - **Threats:** Credential theft and unauthorized device/ user access

   - **Mitigations**

     - Strong identity verification

     - Device identity certificates

     - Dynamic access control policies

     - Use of hardware-rooted trust

6. **Operational security and policies**

   - **Threats:** Insider threats and weak process controls

   - **Mitigations**

     - Security policies and procedures

- Regular audits and compliance checks

- Incident response plans

- Security awareness training

Emerging IoT trends and challenges:

- **Edge Security:** Protecting data processing closer to the device

- **AI and Machine Learning:** Detecting anomalies and threats automatically

- **Supply Chain Security:** Ensuring hardware/software integrity from manufacturing to deployment

- **Regulatory Compliance:** Navigating evolving standards and regulations worldwide

The IoT security landscape is complex and continuously evolving. A holistic approach—covering device, network, data, cloud, and operational security—is essential to safeguard IoT ecosystems and realize their full potential securely.

Table 1-5 shows a summary of the IoT security landscape and its components.

Table 1-5. *IoT Security Landscape and Its Components*

Security area	Focus
Device security	Secure boot, firmware integrity, access control
Network security	Segmentation, VPNs, intrusion detection, encryption (TLS, IPSec)
Application security	Secure APIs, authentication, patching
Cloud security	Data protection, IAM, key management, compliance
Data privacy	GDPR, anonymization, secure data sharing
Identity and access management	Certificates, MFA, privileged access management (PAM)
Monitoring and threat detection	IoT SIEM, anomaly detection, behavioral analytics
Governance and compliance	Standards such as ISO/IEC 30141, ETSI EN 303 645, NISTIR 8259, IEC 62443

Summary

In this chapter, we described the IoT landscapes and major components in security.

We started with the IoT landscape spanning devices, connectivity, data, platforms, and industries, with security and interoperability as the central challenges.

It's a vast and fast-evolving ecosystem connecting the physical and digital worlds.

We introduced in detail IoT environments and at a general level their key components like devices, sensors, actuators, etc.

Then we introduced different types of IoT landscapes from technology and domains point of view. We continued then, by describing more in details some typical IoT architecture landscapes like **Zero Trust Architecture** applied to IoT and IIoT networks, the **Edge-to-Cloud Architecture** (sensors ➤ gateways ➤ cloud ➤ app), the **Mesh Networks** (peer-to-peer device communication), the **Digital Twin Environments** (virtual replica of physical assets), and finally to the **AIoT (Artificial Intelligence of Things)**—AI-driven IoT analytics.

CHAPTER 2

Vulnerabilities in IoT Systems

The Internet of Things (IoT) has revolutionized modern life by connecting billions of devices—ranging from smart home assistants and wearable sensors to industrial machinery and autonomous vehicles. Yet, with this massive connectivity comes a parallel rise in security risks. This chapter examines the full landscape of vulnerabilities in IoT systems, from the hardware level to the global supply chain.

At the **device level**, vulnerabilities often originate from insecure firmware, hardcoded passwords, and outdated software. Many IoT products lack the capability for remote updates or verification of firmware integrity, leaving them perpetually exposed. Hardware weaknesses—such as unprotected debug ports or insecure data storage—further expand the attack surface.

The **network layer** introduces another set of risks. Devices that transmit unencrypted data, maintain open ports, or rely on outdated protocols like Telnet or insecure implementations of MQTT are highly susceptible to interception or hijacking. Weak network segmentation often allows an attacker who compromises one IoT device to infiltrate entire systems.

At the **software and API layer**, flaws in coding and insufficient authentication open new avenues for exploitation. APIs that lack proper authorization controls or input validation can expose sensitive information

© Massimo Nardone 2026
M. Nardone, *Securing Smart Things*, Apress Pocket Guides,
https://doi.org/10.1007/979-8-8688-2367-1_2

or allow attackers to execute unauthorized commands. This is particularly concerning given the widespread use of APIs to bridge IoT devices, cloud services, and user applications.

The chapter also explores **supply chain vulnerabilities**, where risks arise long before a device reaches consumers. Counterfeit components, insecure manufacturing practices, and tampering during distribution can introduce hidden backdoors. As IoT production relies heavily on global suppliers, ensuring trust and traceability throughout the supply chain becomes a crucial security challenge.

Several **real-world case studies** illustrate these concepts vividly. The **Mirai botnet**, which enslaved thousands of IoT devices using default credentials, demonstrates how small oversights can have massive, distributed consequences. Similarly, **smart home breaches** highlight how insecure APIs and weak network protections can directly compromise privacy and physical safety. Industrial IoT incidents reveal that such vulnerabilities can even disrupt manufacturing processes or critical infrastructure

In this chapter, we will describe the following:

- **IoT Systems:** Vulnerable across multiple layers—device, network, software, and supply chain.

- **Device-Level Vulnerabilities:** Stemming from insecure firmware, weak default credentials, and exposed hardware interfaces.

- **Network Vulnerabilities:** Including unencrypted traffic, open ports, and insecure communication protocols like UPnP and MQTT.

- **Software and API Flaws:** Arising from unpatched components, poor authentication, and inadequate data handling.

- **Supply Chain Risks:** That can introduce malicious components or firmware before devices even reach consumers.

- **Case Studies:** The Mirai botnet and smart home breaches illustrate the real-world consequences of poor IoT security.

- **A Security-by-Design Approach:** Emphasizing encryption, authentication, updates, and supply chain integrity is essential to safeguard the IoT ecosystem.

Introduction of IoT Systems

The Internet of Things (IoT) is no longer a futuristic concept—it is an integral part of modern life. From connected cars and smart homes to industrial automation and healthcare devices, IoT systems now form the digital fabric that links people, machines, and data across the world. Yet, for all its innovation and potential, the IoT remains one of the most complex technological ecosystems ever created.

This chapter introduces the concept of IoT systems, exploring their origins, components, architecture, and applications. It sets the stage for deeper discussions about security vulnerabilities, privacy, and resilience in the connected age.

The Internet of Things represents the convergence of the physical and digital worlds. It refers to a vast network of interconnected devices—or "things"—that communicate, collect, and share data through the internet. These devices range from simple sensors that measure temperature or humidity to advanced systems such as autonomous vehicles and industrial robots.

Unlike traditional computers or smartphones, IoT devices are typically embedded into everyday objects, enabling them to sense their environment, make decisions, and interact autonomously. The true power of IoT lies not only in individual devices but in the ecosystem they form—a dynamic, data-driven network that enhances efficiency, automation, and intelligence across every industry.

The Internet of Things (IoT) consists of interconnected devices and sensors that communicate over the internet to automate tasks, collect data, and improve various applications in homes, industries, and cities. As IoT grows, securing these systems becomes crucial to protect data and prevent malicious attacks. IoT typical landscapes are shown in Figure 2-1.

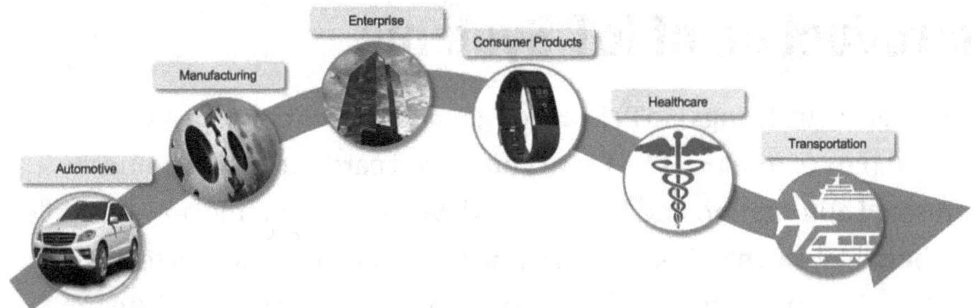

Figure 2-1. *IoT landscapes examples*

The Evolution of IoT

The concept of connected devices dates back decades. In the early 1980s, researchers at Carnegie Mellon University created the first "smart" Coca-Cola vending machine that reported its inventory status over the internet. However, the term **"Internet of Things"** was coined in 1999 by Kevin Ashton, a British technologist working on supply chain optimization using RFID (Radio Frequency Identification) technology.

The early 2000s saw IoT adoption rise alongside advancements in wireless communication, miniaturization of sensors, and the advent of cloud computing. The introduction of IPv6—which vastly expanded the number of possible IP addresses—enabled billions of devices to connect simultaneously. By the 2010s, IoT had evolved into a global phenomenon, driving innovations in smart homes, industrial automation, and healthcare.

The Internet of Things represents one of the most significant technological revolutions of the 21st century. By connecting physical and digital worlds, IoT enables unprecedented levels of automation, efficiency, and intelligence. However, with this transformation comes complexity and risk—from interoperability issues to severe cybersecurity threats.

Understanding the structure, function, and evolution of IoT systems provides the foundation for addressing these challenges. As we progress through this book, the focus will shift toward securing these systems—examining their vulnerabilities, implementing effective defenses, and preparing for the next generation of connected technologies.

Today, IoT systems are foundational to the **Fourth Industrial Revolution**, or **Industry 4.0**, where interconnected cyber-physical systems transform how humans live and work.

Introduction of IoT Security Risks, Targets, Vulnerabilities, and Threat Taxonomy

IoT systems face numerous security risks including unauthorized data access, device hijacking, and service interruptions which can impact individual privacy and critical infrastructure. The primary targets are vulnerable IoT devices, the communication networks they rely on, and cloud-based platforms that process and store data.

Common vulnerabilities include weak authentication mechanisms, insecure firmware updates, unencrypted data transmission, default passwords, and supply chain weaknesses. These vulnerabilities stem from rushed development, limited security expertise, and supply chain complexities.

Threats in IoT can be classified into categories such as malware infections, physical tampering, network exploits, and malicious insider activities. Establishing a clear threat taxonomy helps organizations understand the various attack vectors and develop targeted mitigation strategies to enhance IoT security.

Targets within IoT ecosystems are diverse and include

- **IoT Devices:** Sensors, actuators, smart appliances, and industrial controllers that often operate in unprotected environments

- **Communication Networks:** Wireless protocols like Wi-Fi, Bluetooth, Zigbee, and cellular networks that transmit sensitive data

- **Cloud and Back-end Platforms:** Data processing and storage systems that manage device configurations, user credentials, and operational analytics

Vulnerabilities arise from several core issues:

- **Weak Authentication and Authorization:** Default or hardcoded passwords and lack of multifactor authentication.

- **Insecure Firmware and Software:** Absence of secure update mechanisms, known software bugs, or unpatched vulnerabilities.

- **Unencrypted Data Transmission:** Lack of encryption for data in transit, making interception and eavesdropping trivial.

- **Supply Chain Weaknesses:** Malicious modifications during manufacturing or distribution, including hardware backdoors or compromised components.

- **Limited Security Design:** Cost and resource constraints often lead to minimal security measures during device development.

Threat taxonomy categorizes potential malicious activities:

- **Malware and Ransomware:** Devices infected with malicious software that can be exploited remotely or physically

- **Network Attacks:** Man in the middle (MITM), denial of service (DoS), and port scanning aimed at exploiting network vulnerabilities

- **Physical Tampering:** Attackers gaining access to devices for hardware manipulation or extraction of cryptographic keys

- **Supply Chain Attacks:** Infiltration of malicious components or firmware during manufacturing and distribution, potentially introducing backdoors or vulnerabilities before deployment

- **Insider Threats:** Authorized individuals abusing access to manipulate or extract sensitive information

Understanding this taxonomy aids in recognizing the varied attack vectors and designing comprehensive defense strategies to mitigate risks inherent in IoT deployments.

In the IoT/IIoT environment, what do we need to ensure then?

1. **Protection of data (company, customer, vendor, other)**

2. **Protection of equipment and systems**

3. **Protection against financial loss (assets, brand, company value)**

4. **Compliance with industry regulations**

5. **Increases in reliability, availability, efficiency, and productivity**

6. **Safety inside and outside the operation**

7. **Integration and synergistic alignment of IT and OT practices, policies, and procedures**

8. **Reduce corporate liability/improve enterprise risk management**

9. **Mitigate supply chain risks, both upstream and downstream**

Defining IoT Systems

An **IoT system** is an integrated network of devices, software, and infrastructure that work together to collect, process, and act upon data from the physical world.

At its core, an IoT system performs three main functions:

1. **Sensing:** Capturing real-world data through sensors (e.g., temperature, motion, light, pressure)

2. **Communication:** Transmitting the collected data to other devices, gateways, or cloud platforms

3. **Action:** Processing the data to trigger a response, such as sending alerts, adjusting controls, or automating tasks

For example, a smart irrigation system uses soil moisture sensors (sensing), transmits data via Wi-Fi or cellular networks (communication), and activates sprinklers when needed (action).

The sophistication of IoT lies in how these components integrate—through hardware, connectivity protocols, software applications, and cloud services—to create seamless automation and decision-making systems.

Examples of consumer and industrial IoT systems and devices are shown in Figure 2-2.

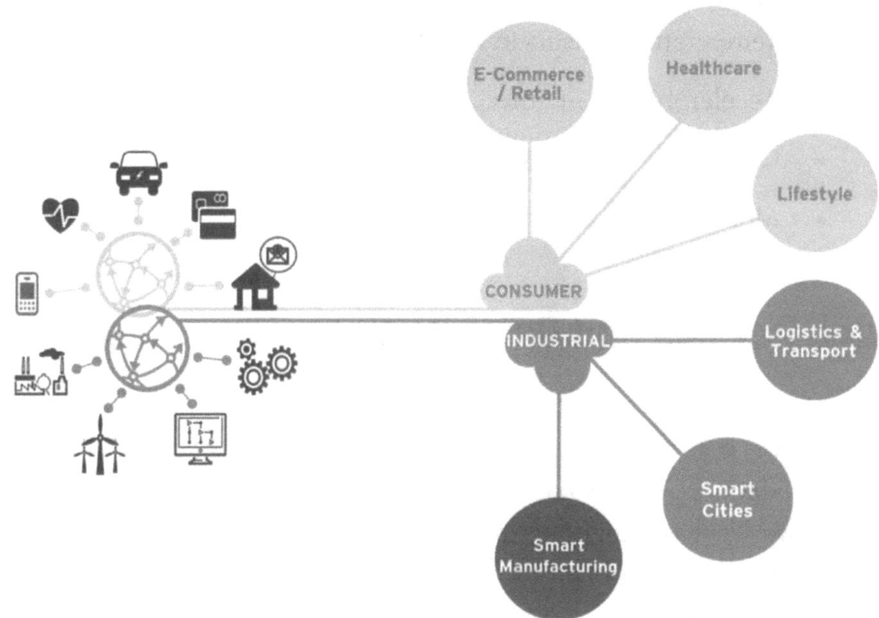

Figure 2-2. *Consumer IoT devices and systems example*

Core Components of IoT Systems

An IoT system is composed of several interconnected layers, each playing a distinct role.

Let's describe the most common IoT systems in use.

Sensors and Actuators

Sensors are the eyes and ears of IoT. They collect data from the environment, such as temperature, pressure, motion, or biometrics. Actuators, on the other hand, perform physical actions based on received instructions—turning on lights, adjusting motors, or opening valves.

Examples:

- Temperature sensors in smart thermostats

- Accelerometers in fitness trackers

- Cameras in security systems

- Motors in robotic arms

Edge Devices and Gateways

Raw data from sensors often requires preprocessing before transmission. Edge devices perform local computations—filtering, aggregating, or analyzing data—to reduce bandwidth and latency.

Gateways act as bridges between local networks and the cloud, handling communication protocols, encryption, and sometimes decision-making at the edge.

Connectivity

Connectivity is the lifeline of IoT systems. Devices communicate using a variety of wired and wireless technologies, depending on power, range, and data requirements.

Common IoT communication standards include

- **Wi-Fi:** High-speed local connectivity for home and office devices

- **Bluetooth/BLE:** Low-power communication for wearables and proximity devices

- **Zigbee/Z-Wave:** Mesh networks for smart homes and industrial environments

- **LoRaWAN:** Long-range, low-power networks for wide-area IoT

- **Cellular (4G/5G):** High-bandwidth communication for mobile or remote systems

Cloud and Data Processing

Once data reaches the cloud, it is stored, processed, and analyzed. Cloud platforms provide scalable resources for data analytics, machine learning, and visualization.

Some IoT systems integrate **edge computing**—processing data closer to where it's generated—to improve response times and reduce cloud dependency.

User Interfaces and Applications

Finally, the processed information is presented to users via dashboards, mobile apps, or automated alerts. These interfaces allow users to monitor systems, make decisions, or control devices remotely.

Architecture of IoT Systems

IoT architectures vary by application but generally follow a **three-layer or five-layer model**.

Three-Layer Model

1. **Perception Layer:** Sensors and actuators that gather data from the environment

2. **Network Layer:** Communication systems that transmit the data

3. **Application Layer:** Software that delivers services to users

Five-Layer Model

1. **Perception Layer:** Physical sensors and data collection mechanisms

2. **Transport Layer:** Data transmission through networks

3. **Processing Layer:** Data storage, analytics, and cloud computing

4. **Application Layer:** Specific services (e.g., smart cities, healthcare)

5. **Business Layer:** System management, revenue models, and business processes

This layered approach provides structure, enabling IoT developers to design systems that are scalable, modular, and secure.

Typical IoT architecture layers and components are shown in Figure 2-3.

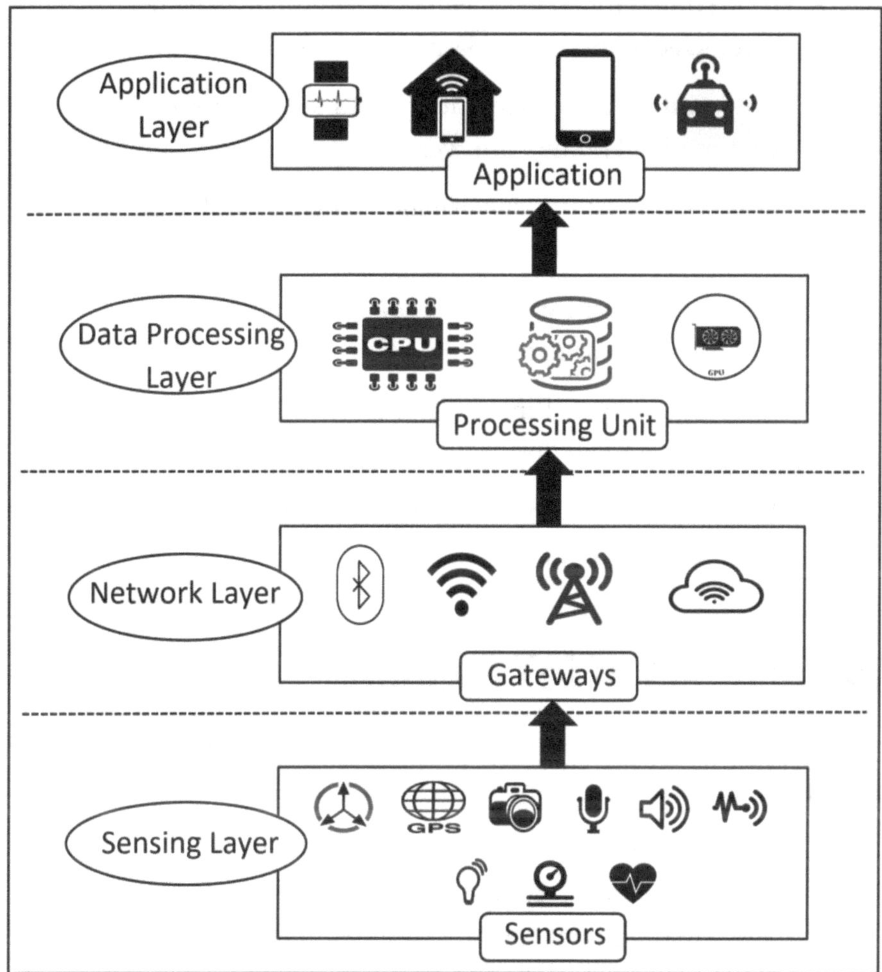

Figure 2-3. *IoT architecture layers and components*

Characteristics of IoT Systems

IoT systems possess several defining characteristics that differentiate them from traditional IT systems:

- **Interconnectivity:** Devices, systems, and people are connected across networks and locations.

- **Automation:** Many operations occur autonomously with minimal human intervention.

- **Scalability:** Systems can expand to include thousands or millions of devices.

- **Context Awareness:** Devices adapt to their environment based on data.

- **Heterogeneity:** IoT integrates a wide variety of devices, protocols, and platforms.

- **Real-Time Operation:** Many IoT applications rely on instantaneous data processing.

Applications of IoT Systems

IoT's versatility has led to its integration across nearly every industry sector including

- **Smart Homes:** Smart homes use IoT-enabled devices to control lighting, temperature, security, and entertainment systems. Examples include smart speakers, thermostats, and door locks.

- **Industrial IoT (IIoT):** In manufacturing and energy, IoT systems optimize operations, reduce downtime, and enable predictive maintenance through real-time equipment monitoring.

- **Healthcare and Wearables:** IoT medical devices track patient vitals, manage chronic conditions, and provide remote diagnostics. Smart wearables measure heart rate, sleep quality, and activity levels.

- **Smart Cities:** Urban IoT applications improve transportation, waste management, public safety, and energy efficiency. Smart traffic lights, for example, adjust in real time to traffic flow.

- **Agriculture:** IoT-driven precision agriculture uses soil sensors, drones, and weather data to optimize irrigation and crop yield.

- **Transportation and Logistics:** Connected vehicles, fleet management systems, and asset-tracking sensors improve supply chain efficiency and safety.

Challenges in IoT Systems

Despite their benefits, IoT systems face critical challenges:

- **Security and Privacy:** Vast numbers of connected devices create large attack surfaces.

- **Interoperability:** Diverse devices and protocols often struggle to communicate seamlessly.

- **Scalability:** Managing massive volumes of data and devices requires advanced infrastructure.

- **Power and Energy Management:** Many IoT devices operate on limited battery life.

- **Regulation and Standardization:** The lack of universal standards complicates deployment and compliance.

These challenges underscore the importance of designing IoT systems that are resilient, interoperable, and secure from the ground up.

What Are the Enterprise IoT Innovators' Top Five Key Challenges?

1. **Unprecedented Data Volumes:** Sensors generating new kinds of data, as well as volumes 1000's of times higher than pre-IoT systems. Big data and machine learning required to complement traditional reporting and analytics.

2. **Fundamental Shifts in Business Models:** One-time purchases being transformed into "pay as you grow" long-term revenue streams. Traditional manufacturing and place-based businesses must become IT-centric organizations.

3. **Incompatible Standards:** Proliferation in competing platforms and incompatible standards raises costs and complexity, security risks, and time-to-market for IoT innovators.

4. **Entirely New Security Threats:** Devices no longer contained and protected in data centers. Automobiles, plants, and medical devices are under growing attack.

5. **New Privacy Landscape:** Collecting physical-world data on people and objects. The market is slow to grasp the implications; stiffer regulations are likely.

Security complexities within IoT environments are unique, and the perception of risk, held by those closest to the issues, needs to be shared by those who approve and manage the IoT/IIoT budget. We must understand the risks, the visibility, and the impacts of IoT.

Risks:

- **Confusion over what is meant by "endpoint" further highlights the need for a reference architecture unique to IIoT.**

- **Lack of risk mitigation and remediation.**

- **Hard to test production environments.**

- **Limited security awareness.**

- **Disparate IT and IoT teams.**

- **Limited patching is done.**

Visibility*:*

- **Limited IoT devices/assets visibility.**

- **Seeing all IoT devices across IoT proprietary protocols is critical.**

- **Operational data and security analytics visibility is limited.**

Impacts:

- **Security incident impact can be catastrophic when IoT Involves OT.**

- **Lack of an IoT security incident response plan and playbook can create significant business disruption.**

- **Customers can lose confidence.**

- **Impact on supply chain partners.**

- **Impact on production.**

- **Legal impact.**

IoT cybersecurity risks might include

- **Physical safety**

- **Productivity and quality control**

- **Data**

- **Reputational and financial**

Let's describe now the most common IoT vulnerabilities which generally include

- **Devices**

- **Applications**

- **Communications technologies**

- **Platforms**

Let's elaborate more the IoT vulnerabilities.

Device-Level Vulnerabilities

At the heart of every IoT network are the devices themselves: the sensors, controllers, and actuators that interact with the physical world. Unfortunately, these devices are often the weakest link in the security chain. Their vulnerabilities usually stem from two areas—firmware and hardware.

Firmware Vulnerabilities

Firmware is the embedded software that runs directly on IoT devices. It dictates how the device operates, communicates, and responds to commands. Many manufacturers, driven by rapid development cycles and competitive pressure, release products with insecure or outdated firmware.

Common problems include devices shipped with **default usernames and passwords,** such as "admin" or "1234," which users rarely change. Attackers can easily exploit these defaults using automated scanning tools. Another widespread issue is the **lack of firmware updates**. Once a product is released, many vendors fail to provide a secure and user-friendly method for updating it, leaving known vulnerabilities unpatched indefinitely.

Equally concerning are **unsigned or unverified firmware updates**. Without digital signatures, an attacker can distribute malicious firmware that appears legitimate. In effect, this allows an adversary to seize total control of the device—often without the user ever realizing something is wrong.

Firmware acts as the foundational software controlling hardware components. Its security is vital; however, many IoT devices suffer from

- **Outdated Firmware:** Manufacturers often do not provide timely updates, leaving devices exposed to known vulnerabilities. For example, the Mirai botnet exploited weak, publicly available credentials on devices with outdated firmware.

- **Insecure Firmware Update Mechanisms:** Without cryptographic signing or encrypted transmission, updates can be intercepted and replaced with malicious versions. Attackers can deploy malicious firmware to gain persistence or control.

- **Hardcoded Secrets and Backdoors:** Some firmware includes hardcoded passwords, encryption keys, or deliberate backdoors, unintentionally or maliciously embedded during manufacturing or by malicious actors infiltrating the development process.

Example: In 2016, researchers demonstrated how vulnerabilities in the firmware of certain IP cameras allowed malicious updates, giving attackers persistent access to the devices.

Secure Firmware Practices

- **Signed and Verified Updates:** All firmware updates should be digitally signed and verified before installation. This ensures that only trusted code runs on the device.

- **Automatic and Secure Update Mechanisms:** Devices should support over-the-air (OTA) updates that are encrypted and authenticated to reduce the window of vulnerability.

- **Elimination of Default Credentials:** Devices must ship with unique credentials, and manufacturers should encourage or enforce password changes upon initial setup.

- **Code Hardening:** Firmware should be developed following secure coding standards, minimizing buffer overflows, injection vulnerabilities, and other common exploits.

Hardware Vulnerabilities

Hardware vulnerabilities can be even harder to detect or fix. They often stem from insecure physical design, inadequate encryption in chips, or overlooked debugging features. Many IoT devices include **open debug**

interfaces, such as JTAG or UART ports, which can be accessed with inexpensive tools. Through these ports, an attacker can extract firmware, read memory, or inject malicious code directly into the device.

There are also **side-channel attacks**, where hackers measure the power consumption or electromagnetic emissions of a device to deduce secret information like encryption keys. And in some cases, sensitive data such as Wi-Fi passwords or API keys are stored **in plaintext** on the device's memory—a critical mistake that allows instant compromise once the hardware is accessed.

Because IoT products are mass-produced at global scale, a single overlooked design flaw can lead to millions of vulnerable devices deployed worldwide.

Hardware vulnerabilities are physical or embedded flaws that an attacker can exploit:

- **Physical Access and Tampering:** Devices deployed in insecure environments—like public spaces or unsupervised facilities—are vulnerable to physical tampering. Attackers can extract firmware, modify hardware components, or implant malicious chips.

- **Embedded Hardware Flaws:** Chips with insecure debugging interfaces, such as UART or JTAG ports left enabled, can be exploited for low-level device control or firmware extraction.

- **Side-Channel Attacks:** These involve analyzing physical signals—such as electromagnetic emissions, power consumption, or timing—to extract secret keys. These attacks are especially relevant in resource-constrained IoT devices with cryptographic functions.

- **Manufacturing Defects:** During assembly, flaws or malicious modifications—such as implanted backdoors—may be introduced. Supply chain risks expand the attack surface by involving third-party manufacturers.

Real-World Example: The Dongle attack demonstrated that some IoT devices contained security backdoors due to manufacturing vulnerabilities, allowing full remote control with little effort.

Hardware Security Measures

- **Secure Boot:** Devices should verify firmware integrity at startup to prevent unauthorized code execution.

- **Hardware Root of Trust:** Embedding cryptographic keys in tamper-resistant hardware ensures that sensitive operations cannot be manipulated externally.

- **Disable Debug Interfaces in Production:** Ports such as JTAG and UART should be disabled or password-protected after development.

- **Secure Data Storage:** Credentials, keys, and sensitive configuration data must be stored encrypted in nonvolatile memory.

Network-Level Vulnerabilities

Even a well-designed device can become vulnerable once it connects to a network. Communication between IoT devices, gateways, and cloud servers often occurs over the internet or local networks—creating an extensive attack surface.

Unencrypted Traffic

One of the most common network-level issues is **unencrypted communication**. Many IoT devices send and receive data in plaintext, meaning that anyone intercepting network traffic can read or modify it. This can include personal data, authentication tokens, or even live camera feeds.

Attackers can perform **man-in-the-middle (MitM)** attacks by inserting themselves between the device and the server, eavesdropping on or altering the communication stream. Without proper use of secure protocols like TLS (Transport Layer Security) or DTLS, the device has no way to verify whether it is communicating with a trusted entity.

Many IoT devices transmit data without proper encryption:

- **Data Interception:** Unencrypted data packets can be captured using simple tools like Wireshark, exposing sensitive personal or operational data.

- **Man-in-the-Middle Attacks (MITM):** Attackers positioned within the network can intercept, modify, or inject malicious data.

- **Impact of Plaintext Protocols:** Protocols such as HTTP, Telnet, or poorly configured MQTT brokers transmit information in plaintext, making eavesdropping trivial. This can lead to compromise of session tokens, credentials, or even firmware updates.

Example: In 2019, researchers exploited unsecured MQTT protocols in smart home devices to spy on occupants and manipulate device states.

Open and Misconfigured Ports

Another major weakness arises from **open network ports**. IoT devices often expose services such as Telnet, SSH, or web dashboards for configuration or maintenance. If these ports are left open to the internet— or protected only by weak credentials—they become easy targets.

Protocols like **Universal Plug and Play (UPnP)** and **MQTT (Message Queuing Telemetry Transport)** are especially risky when misconfigured. UPnP can inadvertently expose internal devices to the outside world, while unsecured MQTT brokers can allow anyone to publish or subscribe to sensitive data streams.

To mitigate such risks, network segmentation, firewall rules, and encrypted communication channels must be enforced at every layer of the IoT architecture.

Software and API Vulnerabilities

Beyond the devices and their networks lies another critical component of IoT ecosystems: the software that binds them together. IoT applications rely heavily on cloud-based services, web interfaces, and APIs. Each of these elements presents unique vulnerabilities.

Insecure Software Components

Developers often build IoT firmware and applications using **open source libraries** or third-party components. While this speeds up development, it also introduces dependency risks. Outdated or unpatched software modules can become gateways for attackers. A vulnerable SSL library or embedded web server, for instance, can lead to **remote code execution** or unauthorized access.

Some devices even reuse the same base code across multiple models or brands, amplifying the scale of any discovered vulnerability.

API Vulnerabilities

Application programming interfaces (APIs) are the connective tissue of IoT systems. They allow mobile apps and cloud platforms to communicate with devices, fetch data, and issue commands. But when APIs are insecure, they become a goldmine for attackers.

Common API vulnerabilities include **missing authentication or authorization checks**, which allow anyone to access data that should be private. Others expose **excessive data**—for example, returning full device configurations when only a simple status update is needed.

Poorly designed APIs can also lack **rate limiting**, making them vulnerable to brute-force attacks or denial-of-service conditions. To protect IoT ecosystems, developers must treat APIs with the same rigor as any critical software component—implementing authentication tokens, encryption, and input validation at every stage.

Supply Chain and Manufacturing Vulnerabilities

IoT devices rarely come from a single source. Their components—chips, sensors, firmware, and software—are often sourced from a global network of suppliers. While this supply chain enables innovation and lower costs, it also introduces significant security challenges.

Counterfeit and Tampered Components

A compromised or counterfeit component can introduce vulnerabilities at the hardware level. Malicious chips, embedded backdoors, or tampered firmware can be inserted during manufacturing, often without the knowledge of the final device maker. Once deployed, these devices may leak data or allow remote control without any visible signs of compromise.

Insecure Production Environments

Even legitimate manufacturers can fall victim to cyberattacks targeting their **production environments**. A compromised build system or firmware signing process can lead to entire product lines being shipped with malware preinstalled. Such incidents have occurred across multiple industries, from consumer electronics to industrial automation.

Lack of Provenance Tracking

Finally, many manufacturers lack **traceability** in their supply chains. Without proper provenance tracking—such as digital certificates or blockchain-based verification—it becomes nearly impossible to confirm whether a device or component is authentic and secure.

To mitigate these risks, organizations must adopt end-to-end supply chain security practices, including vendor audits, secure firmware signing, and post-deployment integrity checks.

IoT cybersecurity point of attack and vulnerabilities are shown in Figure 2-4.

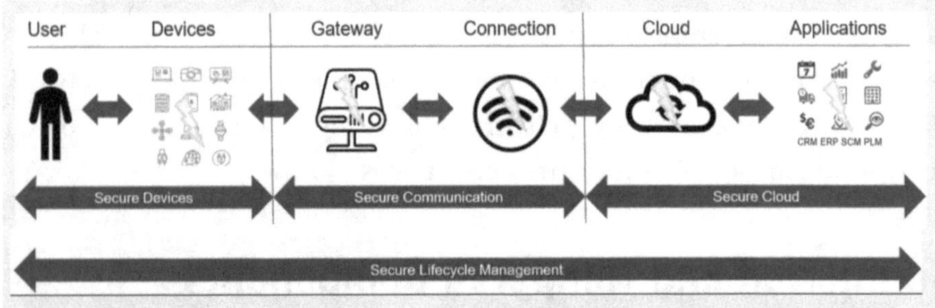

Figure 2-4. *IoT cybersecurity point of attack and vulnerabilities*

Examples of IoT Botnet and Breaches

Let's describe now a real-world case study: the Mirai botnet.

In 2016, the **Mirai botnet** revealed the terrifying potential of insecure IoT devices. The malware scanned the internet for devices using default login credentials—targeting routers, IP cameras, and DVRs. Once infected, these devices became part of a massive botnet capable of launching distributed denial-of-service (DDoS) attacks.

Mirai's power was staggering. At its peak, it disrupted major websites and services, including Twitter, Netflix, and Amazon Web Services. The incident highlighted how something as simple as a factory-set password could lead to a global-scale cyberattack.

Mirai served as a wake-up call for the industry, demonstrating that IoT security must be built in from the start rather than bolted on after deployment.

Smart Home Breaches

The rise of smart homes has introduced new layers of risk to everyday life. Reports have surfaced of hackers gaining control of baby monitors, smart locks, and home security cameras. In many cases, the root cause was shockingly simple: **weak passwords**, **unencrypted traffic**, or **exposed APIs**.

One particularly unsettling trend involves unauthorized access to smart cameras, where attackers have been able to view or even speak through compromised devices. These breaches underscore a critical point—when security fails in IoT, the consequences are not just digital but deeply personal.

IoT Security Standards

Adherence to these standards ensures that IoT devices and systems incorporate fundamental security controls. It promotes interoperability between devices from different manufacturers, reduces security gaps, and builds user trust.

Why Standards Matter?

Adhering to established standards fosters

- **Interoperability:** Ensures devices can communicate securely regardless of manufacturer

- **Security Assurance:** Provides confidence to users and regulators that devices meet baseline security requirements

- **Regulatory Compliance:** Meets emerging legal frameworks and industry regulations

- **Risk Reduction:** Minimizes vulnerabilities proactively rather than reacting to breaches

Here is an in-depth overview of key IoT security standards.

IEC 62443 Series

- **Scope and Purpose:** Developed by the International Electrotechnical Commission (IEC), the IEC 62443 series provides comprehensive cybersecurity standards for industrial automation and control systems (IACS), which overlap significantly with IoT applications in critical infrastructure.

- **Key features**

  - Risk assessment methodologies tailored for industrial environments

  - Security life cycle management, from design to decommissioning

  - Requirements for network and system security architecture

  - Implementation of secure communication protocols and access controls

- **Impact:** Adoption of IEC 62443 helps industrial organizations build resilient and secure control systems, preventing sabotage, data theft, and operational disruptions.

ISO/IEC 30141:2018 (IoT Reference Architecture)

- **Scope and Purpose:** Provides a holistic blueprint for designing IoT systems with embedded security, privacy, and interoperability considerations

- **Key features**

  - Defines functional components such as devices, gateways, cloud services, and communication networks

  - Emphasizes security features like device identity, authentication, and data integrity

  - Promotes privacy-by-design, ensuring user data is protected throughout the data life cycle

- **Impact:** Guides manufacturers and developers in building secure, scalable, and interoperable IoT solutions

IEEE 802.1AR (Secure Device Identity)

- **Scope and Purpose:** Focuses on establishing a trusted identity for IoT devices through a robust security-enhanced device identity standard

- **Key features**

  - Secure enrollment and provisioning of devices

  - Use of cryptographic credentials (e.g., X.509 certificates)

  - Enables mutual authentication between devices and networks

- **Impact:** Prevents device impersonation and unauthorized access, forming the basis for secure device onboarding

NISTIR 8228 (IoT Cybersecurity Capability Core Baseline)

- **Scope and Purpose:** Provides guidance for creating a minimum cybersecurity baseline for IoT devices, emphasizing practical measures

- **Key features**

  - Hardware security practices, such as tamper resistance

  - Secure boot and firmware integrity checks

  - Encryption for communication channels

  - Robust authentication mechanisms

- **Impact:** Serves as a practical reference guide for manufacturers and developers aiming for secure IoT device deployment.

Summary

Internet of Things (IoT) systems have become integral to modern life, enabling seamless connectivity across households, industries, and cities. However, the rapid proliferation of IoT devices has also introduced a wide array of security vulnerabilities. This chapter delves into the multifaceted nature of IoT vulnerabilities, examining device-level issues, network risks, software weaknesses, supply chain concerns, and real-world case studies.

We introduced in detail the most common IoT vulnerabilities like device-level, network-level, software and API, etc.

We also described in this chapter the **IoT systems** that connect physical devices, software, and cloud infrastructure to collect and act on real-world data as well as the ecosystem that includes **sensors, edge devices, gateways, networks, cloud platforms,** and **user interfaces.**

Also, **different core architectures** ranging from three-layer to five-layer models, emphasizing perception, communication, and application, were explained.

We discussed why these days vulnerabilities in IoT systems span from hardware to software to network infrastructure and how addressing these requires a comprehensive security approach that includes secure device design, regular updates, encrypted communications, supply chain integrity, and user education.

Finally, we provided an in-depth overview of key IoT security standards, including IEC 62443 Series, ISO/IEC 30141:2018, NISTIR 8228, etc.

CHAPTER 3

Threats and Cybersecurity Attack Vectors for IoT

The Internet of Things (IoT) is reshaping the technological landscape by connecting billions of devices, allowing them to collect, exchange, and act on data autonomously. While this connectivity offers unparalleled convenience and efficiency, it also presents significant security challenges. IoT devices are often deployed with minimal security measures, making them prime targets for cyber threats.

One of the primary threats to IoT systems is unauthorized access. Attackers exploit weak authentication mechanisms, such as default passwords or insecure credentials, to gain control over devices. Once accessed, these devices can be used as entry points into broader networks, leading to data breaches or enabling espionage.

Another prevalent threat is the use of malware, specifically tailored to exploit IoT vulnerabilities. The infamous Mirai botnet is a prime example, where malware infected a vast number of IoT devices to launch distributed denial-of-service (DDoS) attacks, crippling major internet services.

Network-based attacks, like man-in-the-middle (MITM) attacks, are also common. Without proper encryption, data transmitted between IoT devices can be intercepted and altered, leading to unauthorized manipulation of device operations or data leakage.

© Massimo Nardone 2026
M. Nardone, *Securing Smart Things*, Apress Pocket Guides,
https://doi.org/10.1007/979-8-8688-2367-1_3

Physical tampering remains a tangible risk, especially for devices located in unsecured or public environments. Attackers can gain physical access to hack devices, extract sensitive data, or inject malicious code.

Additionally, IoT devices face threats from poor software and firmware security. Unpatched vulnerabilities, code injection, and insecure APIs can lead to device compromise. Attackers exploit these weaknesses to execute arbitrary code or disrupt operations.

The supply chain introduces further vulnerabilities, where malicious actors can embed backdoors or tamper with devices during manufacturing and distribution.

To mitigate these threats, a multilayered cybersecurity strategy is essential. This includes implementing robust encryption, ensuring secure device onboarding and management, maintaining up-to-date software, and applying network security protocols. By understanding and addressing these threats, stakeholders can enhance the resilience and trustworthiness of IoT systems.

This chapter will discuss about various threats and attack vectors targeting IoT systems, highlighting the need for comprehensive cybersecurity measures.

The chapter will discuss about the following:

- Threat actor **motivations and tactics** (APT groups, cybercrime economics, insider psychology)

- Detailed **technical mechanics** of each attack (how DDoS, MitM, ransomware, and botnets actually work in IoT environments)

- Expanded **emerging threats** (AI weaponization, deepfake IoT data, quantum threats, edge AI exploitation)

- Additional **case studies**—including attacks like
  BrickerBot, SolarWinds, and Colonial Pipeline

- Comprehensive **risk assessment models**, **attack
  surface taxonomy**, and **mitigation frameworks** (e.g.,
  NIST, ISO/IEC 30141)

Introduction

In the modern era of hyperconnectivity, the Internet of Things (IoT) has
revolutionized the way individuals, organizations, and nations interact
with technology. From industrial automation to healthcare, smart
cities, and consumer electronics, IoT systems now form the invisible
infrastructure that drives digital transformation. Yet, the same connectivity
that empowers innovation also amplifies exposure to a vast and complex
spectrum of cybersecurity threats. IoT devices—ranging from simple
sensors to autonomous vehicles—represent billions of potential entry
points for malicious actors. Their diversity, resource constraints, and
often limited built-in security make them particularly susceptible to
exploitation.

Cybersecurity within IoT environments is not merely a technical
challenge but a systemic risk that impacts privacy, safety, and even
national security. The convergence of physical and digital systems means
that an attack against an IoT network can transcend the cyber realm
and cause tangible, real-world harm. For instance, the compromise of a
smart thermostat may seem trivial, but similar vulnerabilities in medical
implants, autonomous cars, or power grids can result in catastrophic
outcomes. Thus, understanding the nature of threats and attack vectors
targeting IoT ecosystems is a critical prerequisite for developing robust
defense mechanisms.

This chapter explores the evolving landscape of cybersecurity threats and attack vectors in IoT systems. It begins by examining the major categories of threat actors—hackers, nation-states, insiders, and hacktivists—before delving into the common types of attacks such as distributed denial of service (DDoS), man in the middle (MitM), and ransomware. It then investigates emerging threat vectors, including artificial intelligence (AI)-driven attacks and manipulation of edge devices. Real-world case studies, such as the Mirai botnet and Jeep Cherokee hack, provide concrete insights into the devastating potential of these threats. Finally, the chapter concludes with a comprehensive discussion on risk assessment and attack surface analysis, offering strategies for enhancing resilience in the IoT ecosystem.

Figure 3-1 shows a defense in depth example approach of the mitigation techniques throughout the life cycle of an IoT device.

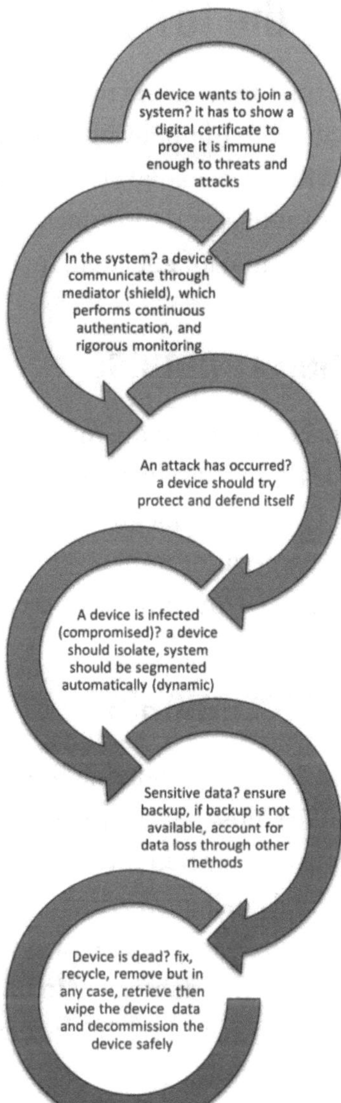

Figure 3-1. *Mitigation techniques throughout the life cycle of an IoT device*

Threat Actors in the IoT Ecosystem

In the cybersecurity domain, threat actors represent individuals, organizations, or groups that intentionally or unintentionally cause harm to information systems. Within the IoT landscape, these actors vary widely in motivation, technical expertise, and resources. Understanding their intent and capabilities is essential for effective threat modeling.

Hackers and Cybercriminals

Hackers and cybercriminals are among the most common threat actors. They exploit vulnerabilities in IoT systems for financial gain, reputation, or intellectual challenge. Cybercriminal groups often target consumer IoT devices—such as security cameras or routers—to create large botnets for distributed denial-of-service (DDoS) attacks or cryptocurrency mining.

Hackers and Cybercriminals

Hackers—ranging from independent individuals to organized cybercrime groups—represent one of the most persistent and adaptive categories of threat actors. Their motivations often revolve around financial gain, notoriety, or intellectual challenge. Within IoT environments, hackers exploit weaknesses such as outdated firmware, unencrypted communications, and exposed interfaces to gain unauthorized access. Once inside a system, they may steal data, hijack devices for botnets, or install ransomware to extort victims.

Cybercriminal organizations have industrialized this process, creating a black-market economy around IoT exploitation. Malware-as-a-service (MaaS) and botnet rental services enable less-skilled individuals to launch sophisticated attacks with minimal effort. For example, the infamous **Mirai botnet**, which leveraged thousands of insecure IoT devices to launch one of the largest DDoS attacks in history, originated from the efforts of relatively low-skilled hackers using automated tools. This case demonstrates that even basic vulnerabilities, when scaled across millions of devices, can result in massive global disruptions.

Nation-States and Cyberwarfare

Nation-states possess significant resources and advanced cyber capabilities. Their objectives often include espionage, sabotage, or disruption of critical infrastructure. IoT systems in energy, transportation, and defense sectors are particularly vulnerable to nation-state attacks, which may use custom-built malware and zero-day exploits. The Stuxnet worm, which targeted Iran's nuclear facilities, remains one of the most sophisticated examples of nation-state cyber operations.

Nation-state actors represent the most advanced and well-funded threat group. Their objectives often include espionage, sabotage, or geopolitical influence. State-sponsored cyber operations increasingly target IoT systems because they provide access to critical infrastructure, defense assets, and sensitive data. The **Stuxnet worm**, for instance, showcased how cyberweapons could cross the boundary between the digital and physical worlds by targeting industrial control systems (ICS) within Iran's nuclear facilities.

Nation-state attacks are characterized by their persistence, complexity, and precision. These actors employ Advanced Persistent Threats (APTs), which infiltrate networks and remain undetected for extended periods. In the IoT context, this may involve compromising sensors in energy grids, manipulating telemetry data from satellites, or installing covert surveillance tools in consumer devices. The geopolitical implications are profound: control over IoT-based infrastructure can translate directly into strategic dominance in both war and peace.

Insiders and Negligent Employees

Insider threats include employees, contractors, or partners who have legitimate access to systems but misuse their privileges. These individuals may act maliciously or inadvertently compromise IoT networks through poor security practices, such as using weak passwords or connecting unauthorized devices.

While much attention is focused on external attackers, insiders pose a particularly insidious threat. Employees, contractors, or partners with legitimate access to systems can intentionally or accidentally cause severe damage. In the context of IoT, an insider might leak credentials, tamper with firmware updates, or disable security controls for convenience. Because IoT systems often span multiple organizations and supply chains, insiders may exploit gaps in accountability to conceal malicious activities.

Unintentional insider threats are equally dangerous. Negligence— such as failing to apply updates, using weak passwords, or connecting unauthorized devices—can create vulnerabilities that external attackers later exploit. As IoT deployments expand into smart factories, connected healthcare, and critical infrastructure, insider awareness and governance become essential components of any security framework.

Hacktivists and Competitors

Hacktivist groups target organizations to promote social or political causes, often using IoT vulnerabilities to deface systems or leak data. Competitors may also engage in corporate espionage, attempting to extract proprietary information from IoT-enabled manufacturing or logistics systems.

Hacktivists—motivated by political or ideological goals—target IoT systems to promote social causes or disrupt entities they oppose. Their actions may include defacing connected digital signage, exposing sensitive data, or disabling smart city services to draw public attention. Though less resourced than nation-states, hacktivists can still cause considerable reputational and financial damage through coordinated campaigns.

Corporate espionage also manifests in IoT environments. Competitors may deploy advanced surveillance or data exfiltration techniques to gain insights into proprietary processes. Industrial IoT (IIoT) systems are particularly vulnerable since they contain valuable operational data and intellectual property. The blurring of lines between corporate competition and cyber conflict adds another layer of complexity to the IoT threat landscape.

Figure 3-2 shows a view of the IoT threat impacts.

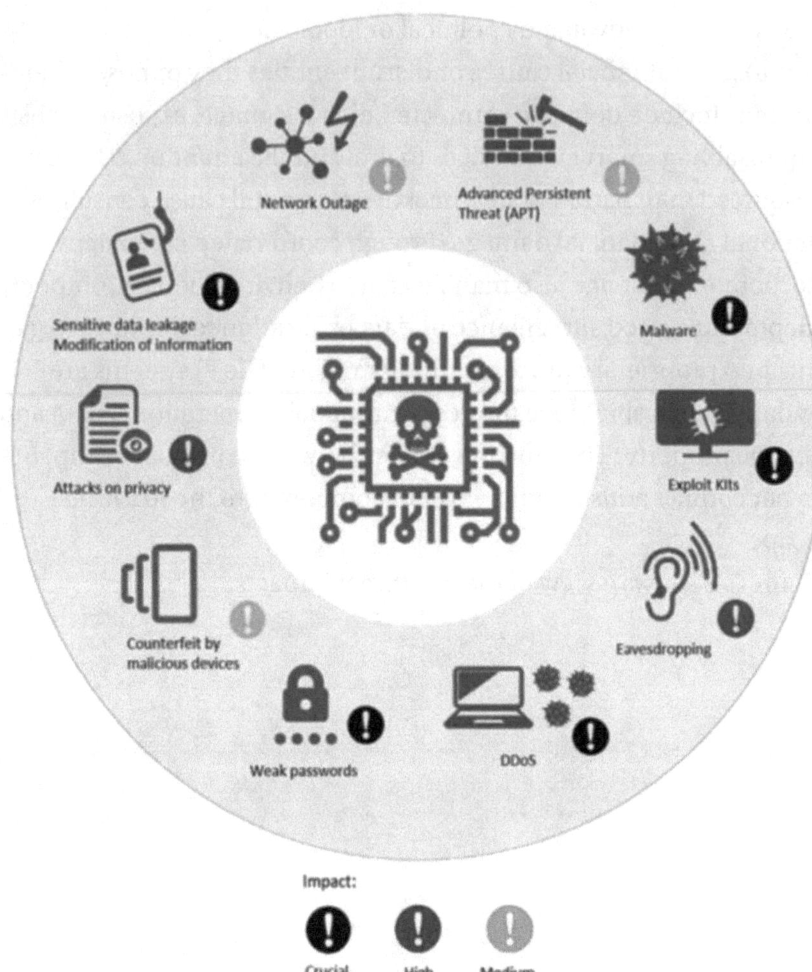

Figure 3-2. *A view of IoT threat impacts*

Common Cyberattacks Targeting IoT Systems

The diversity of IoT systems—from personal devices in homes and healthcare to critical infrastructure and connected vehicles—makes them all potential targets for cyberattacks. As these systems become more integral to daily life and essential services, the consequences of their compromise escalate dramatically—ranging from privacy violations to physical harm and societal disruptions

IoT systems targeted by cyberattacks span from households and automobiles to critical infrastructure and industrial environments. Vehicles, in particular, are increasingly vulnerable as they connect more systems online, making them a prime target for malicious control or espionage. Protecting these systems requires tailored security measures that consider their specific use cases and operational environments.

Here's a more detailed elaboration on the systems targeted by cyberattacks:

1. **Smart home devices**

   Smart home technology has become ubiquitous, providing convenience and improved security. However, its growing popularity makes these devices attractive cyber targets. Attackers exploit vulnerabilities to gain unauthorized access, leading to privacy breaches and physical security risks.

   - **Examples**

     - **Security Cameras:** Once compromised, attackers can view live feeds or record footage, invading privacy.

- **Smart Locks:** Unauthorized access can unlock doors, leading to burglaries.

- **Voice Assistants (e.g., Alexa, Google Home):** Hijacking these devices can enable attackers to eavesdrop or control connected systems.

- **Smart Thermostats and Appliances:** Manipulation could cause discomfort or damage electronics.

- **Impact:** Data theft, privacy violations, physical unauthorized access, and even physical harm if security breaches disable locks or alarms.

2. **Industrial control systems (ICS) and Supervisory Control and Data Acquisition (SCADA)**

   Industrial IoT (IIoT) seeks to automate manufacturing, utilities, and infrastructure management. These systems are prime targets due to their criticality.

   - **Examples**

     - Power grids, water treatment plants, manufacturing robots, oil and gas facilities

     - Remote sensors that monitor system health, flow, or pressure

   - **Targeted attacks**

     - **Disruption of Critical Services:** Plant shutdowns, blackouts, or pipe leakages

     - **Sabotage:** Deliberate manipulation leading to physical damage or environmental hazards

- **Data Theft:** Stealing operational data or trade secrets

- **Impact:** Disruption of essential services, safety risks, environmental hazards, economic losses, and potential threats to public safety

3. **Connected vehicles and automotive systems**

Modern vehicles are increasingly connected, with integrated IoT components such as infotainment, navigation, and diagnostics.

- **Examples**

  - **Infotainment Systems and Telematics:** Can be exploited to access personal data or inject malicious commands

  - **Engine Control Units (ECUs):** Vulnerable to remote hacking, potentially allowing control over acceleration, braking, or steering

  - **Autonomous Vehicles:** Pose significant safety risks if malicious actors manipulate their sensors or control algorithms

- **Targeted attacks**

  - **Remote Control Hijacking:** Causing accidents or steering off-road

  - **Data Theft:** Personal data, driving patterns, or location info

  - **Physical Safety Risks:** Threats to driver, passengers, and pedestrians

- **Impact:** Physical harm, privacy violations, vehicle theft, or systemic disruptions in transportation infrastructure

4. **Healthcare IoT devices**

   Medical IoT devices enhance patient care but also pose privacy and safety risks if compromised.

   - **Examples**

     - **Wearables:** Fitness trackers and health monitors transmitting sensitive health data

     - **Hospital Equipment:** Infusion pumps, defibrillators, and remote monitoring systems

   - **Targeted attacks**

     - **Data Breaches:** Stealing sensitive personal health information

     - **Device Manipulation:** Altering medication dosages or disabling life-support equipment

     - **Interference with Treatments:** Disrupting continuous monitoring, risking patient safety

   - **Impact:** Privacy violations, compromised patient safety, legal liabilities, and loss of trust

5. **Smart city and public infrastructure**

   Urban environments increasingly utilize IoT for transportation, lighting, surveillance, and environmental monitoring.

   - **Examples**

     - Traffic control systems, smart streetlights, public Wi-Fi, air quality sensors

- **Targeted attacks**

  - **Traffic Disruption:** Causing congestion or accidents by hacking traffic lights

  - **Public Safety Hazards:** Disabling surveillance or emergency systems

  - **Data Privacy:** Breaching citizen data collected for urban planning

- **Impact:** Disruption of city operations, safety threats, and erosion of public trust

6. **Retail and payment systems**

   IoT facilitates checkout-free shopping, inventory management, and customer engagement.

   - **Examples**

     - Smart kiosks, RFID inventory systems, connected POS terminals

   - **Targeted attacks**

     - **Data Theft:** Stealing payment info and customer data

     - **Manipulation of Inventory Data:** Causing stock inaccuracies, theft, or fraud

     - **Service Disruption:** Interfering with checkout systems or supply chain tracking

   - **Impact:** Financial losses, reputational damage, and customer data breaches

Figure 3-3 shows the most common cyberattacks targeting IoT systems.

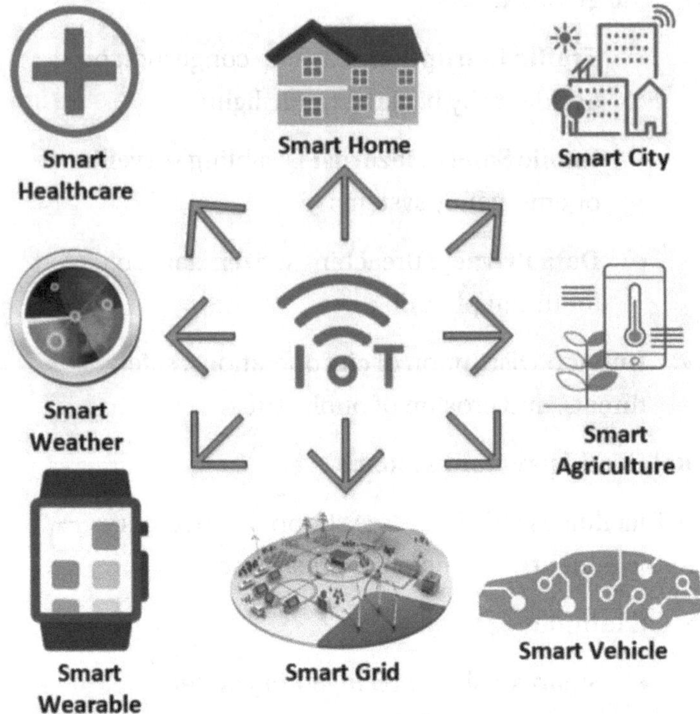

Figure 3-3. *Most common cyberattacks targeting IoT systems*

Cybersecurity Attack Types Targeting IoT Devices

IoT systems face a broad range of cyber threats that exploit their distributed nature and frequent lack of robust security controls.

The following sections describe the most prevalent attack types targeting IoT devices and networks.

Distributed Denial of Service (DDoS)

A distributed denial-of-service attack aims to overwhelm a target's network or services with excessive traffic, rendering them unavailable to legitimate users. In IoT environments, attackers often compromise thousands or even millions of devices to create massive botnets capable of generating terabits of malicious traffic. The **Mirai botnet**, for example, used insecure IoT devices such as webcams and routers to take down major websites including Twitter, Netflix, and Reddit in 2016.

The underlying reason IoT devices are effective in DDoS attacks lies in their simplicity and connectivity. Many are configured with hardcoded credentials and rarely updated, allowing attackers to automate large-scale compromises. Once infected, devices continuously send requests to targeted servers, consuming bandwidth and computing resources. Defending against DDoS attacks in IoT systems requires layered approaches such as traffic filtering, rate limiting, anomaly detection, and cloud-based mitigation services.

Man-in-the-Middle (MitM) Attacks

MitM attacks occur when an adversary intercepts and potentially alters communications between two IoT devices or between a device and the cloud. This can lead to data theft, manipulation of sensor readings, or injection of malicious commands. Unencrypted communication channels and weak authentication mechanisms make IoT networks particularly susceptible to such attacks.

Man-in-the-middle attacks occur when an adversary intercepts communication between two entities—such as a sensor and a control system—without their knowledge. This allows the attacker to eavesdrop, modify, or inject data packets, thereby compromising confidentiality and integrity. In IoT environments, unencrypted or poorly secured communication protocols like MQTT, CoAP, or HTTP are especially vulnerable.

A common example is when attackers set up rogue access points that mimic legitimate Wi-Fi networks. When IoT devices connect, the attacker can manipulate transmitted data, replay commands, or inject malicious payloads. In industrial settings, this could lead to false readings or unauthorized control over machinery. Preventing MitM attacks requires the use of strong encryption (TLS/SSL), certificate-based authentication, and network segmentation to isolate sensitive communications.

Malware and Ransomware

Malware targeting IoT systems has evolved from simple worms to sophisticated ransomware. Attackers can encrypt the firmware or configuration files of IoT devices, demanding payment for decryption keys. In industrial IoT settings, ransomware can halt operations, resulting in severe financial and operational damage.

Malware and ransomware have evolved from targeting computers and smartphones to compromising IoT devices. Once an IoT system is infected, attackers can disrupt operations, exfiltrate data, or lock devices until a ransom is paid. The challenge lies in the fact that many IoT devices lack sufficient memory and processing power to run advanced security software, making detection and recovery extremely difficult.

For example, in 2020, a wave of ransomware attacks targeted connected medical devices in hospitals, disrupting patient care and diagnostics. Attackers exploited unpatched vulnerabilities in hospital networks and IoT endpoints. Beyond financial loss, such attacks pose ethical and safety concerns—malicious interference with medical devices or autonomous vehicles could endanger human lives. To counter ransomware, organizations must employ frequent firmware updates, strict network access controls, and secure data backup strategies.

Data Breaches and Credential Theft

Many IoT devices store sensitive data such as user credentials, sensor readings, or operational parameters. Weak storage encryption and insecure APIs can allow attackers to exfiltrate this data, leading to privacy violations and identity theft.

Data breaches are among the most common cybersecurity incidents affecting IoT systems. Because IoT devices often collect sensitive data—such as user behavior, geolocation, or biometric information—they become attractive targets for identity theft and surveillance. Attackers exploit weak authentication schemes, default credentials, and unencrypted data storage to exfiltrate valuable information.

The **Verkada camera breach** in 2021 is a prime example, where hackers gained access to live feeds from over 150,000 security cameras deployed in hospitals, schools, and corporate offices. By exploiting exposed administrative credentials, they were able to infiltrate Verkada's cloud infrastructure. The incident revealed how central management platforms, while convenient, can become single points of failure in IoT ecosystems.

Botnets and Remote Code Execution

IoT botnets consist of compromised devices that can be remotely controlled to perform coordinated attacks. Remote code execution vulnerabilities enable attackers to gain full control over devices, install malware, or use them for lateral movement across networks.

IoT botnets are networks of compromised devices controlled remotely by an attacker. These botnets can be rented, sold, or used for various malicious purposes such as spamming, credential stuffing, or distributed attacks. The **BrickerBot** malware, for instance, went a step further by permanently disabling vulnerable IoT devices through destructive commands, effectively creating "digital paperweights."

Remote code execution (RCE) vulnerabilities enable attackers to inject and run malicious code on IoT devices. Such exploits often stem from insecure APIs, improper input validation, or outdated libraries. Once inside, attackers can pivot through the network, escalate privileges, and gain full control over connected systems. Mitigating these risks requires rigorous code audits, secure development practices, and robust patch management policies.

Emerging Threat Vectors

As IoT technology evolves, so do the methods used by attackers. Emerging threat vectors leverage artificial intelligence, edge computing, and complex supply chains to exploit previously overlooked weaknesses.

As technology evolves, so too do the methods of attack. Traditional cybersecurity measures are increasingly challenged by sophisticated and adaptive threat vectors. The convergence of AI, edge computing, and 5G connectivity introduces both opportunities and vulnerabilities in IoT systems.

AI-Powered Cyberattacks

Artificial intelligence has become a double-edged sword in cybersecurity. While defenders use AI for anomaly detection and automated threat response, attackers also leverage AI to enhance their capabilities. AI-powered malware can autonomously identify weak targets, adapt to changing environments, and evade traditional defenses. Such attacks may involve self-learning botnets that evolve over time, making detection and mitigation more difficult.

Moreover, AI enables large-scale social engineering campaigns. Deepfake audio and video can impersonate legitimate operators in industrial control environments or manipulate sensor data to create false perceptions. The weaponization of AI poses unprecedented challenges, as attacks become faster, smarter, and harder to trace.

Edge Device Manipulation

With the rise of edge computing, data processing increasingly occurs closer to the source—on IoT gateways, edge servers, and devices themselves. This decentralization reduces latency but also creates new attack surfaces. Edge devices often operate outside centralized security oversight, making them attractive targets for manipulation.

Attackers may compromise edge nodes to alter data before it reaches the cloud, inject malware into local AI models, or conduct lateral movement across distributed systems. For instance, altering sensor readings in smart manufacturing could disrupt production quality, while tampering with traffic data in smart cities could cause real-world chaos. Securing the edge requires encryption at all levels, continuous monitoring, and tamper-resistant hardware designs.

Adversarial Machine Learning

Adversarial machine learning (AML) involves crafting deceptive inputs that cause AI models to make incorrect decisions. In IoT applications— such as facial recognition, autonomous navigation, or predictive maintenance—this could have serious consequences. Attackers might subtly alter an image or sensor input so that an AI model misclassifies an object, leading to accidents or system failures.

An example occurred when researchers demonstrated that a few stickers placed on a stop sign could cause an autonomous vehicle's vision system to misidentify it as a speed limit sign. This highlights the fragility of AI-driven IoT systems and the need for robust model validation and adversarial training.

Supply Chain and Firmware Poisoning

IoT devices often rely on complex supply chains that include multiple vendors and third-party software components. Attackers exploit these dependencies to inject malicious code during manufacturing or firmware updates—a tactic known as supply chain poisoning. The **SolarWinds breach** illustrated how attackers could compromise software supply chains to infiltrate thousands of organizations simultaneously.

Firmware poisoning in IoT systems can have long-term consequences, as compromised devices may remain undetected for years. Ensuring integrity across supply chains requires strict vendor verification, cryptographic signing of firmware, and continuous monitoring for anomalous behavior.

Real-World Case Studies

Real incidents provide tangible evidence of how cyber threats exploit IoT vulnerabilities. This section explores several high-profile cases that have shaped the modern understanding of IoT security risks.

The Mirai Botnet (2016)

The Mirai botnet is one of the most infamous IoT-based cyberattacks in history. Created by exploiting default usernames and passwords on consumer devices like routers and cameras, Mirai assembled a massive botnet capable of launching DDoS attacks exceeding 1 terabit per second. The attack on Dyn DNS disrupted major platforms including Twitter, Spotify, and GitHub, demonstrating how consumer-grade devices could destabilize global internet services. Mirai's source code was later released publicly, spawning countless variants and making IoT security a mainstream concern.

Stuxnet: Cyber-Physical Warfare

Stuxnet marked the first known instance of a cyberweapon designed to cause physical destruction. Believed to be developed by nation-state actors, it targeted Iran's nuclear enrichment facilities by infecting programmable logic controllers (PLCs). The malware subtly altered centrifuge speeds while feeding operators false data, leading to significant physical damage. Stuxnet proved that cyberattacks could transcend virtual boundaries, introducing the era of cyber-physical warfare and forever changing the landscape of industrial IoT security.

The Verkada Smart Camera Breach (2021)

Hackers gained access to Verkada's cloud-based security camera system, viewing live feeds from over 150,000 cameras across high-profile clients. The attackers exploited exposed administrative credentials, demonstrating the risks of centralized IoT management platforms. The breach raised ethical and legal questions about surveillance, privacy, and vendor responsibility in cloud-connected IoT ecosystems.

Jeep Cherokee Hack (2015)

Security researchers Charlie Miller and Chris Valasek demonstrated how a remote attacker could control a Jeep Cherokee via its infotainment system. They exploited vulnerabilities in the vehicle's Wi-Fi and cellular interfaces to manipulate steering, brakes, and transmission. This event prompted a massive vehicle recall and underscored the critical importance of securing automotive IoT systems.

The Colonial Pipeline Incident (2021)

Although primarily a ransomware attack, the Colonial Pipeline breach illustrated how interconnected IT and IoT systems could disrupt national infrastructure. Attackers infiltrated IT networks, forcing a shutdown of the operational technology (OT) systems controlling fuel distribution. The resulting fuel shortages across the United States highlighted the vulnerabilities of critical infrastructure reliant on digital control systems.

Risk Assessment and Attack Surface Analysis

Risk assessment is a systematic process for identifying, evaluating, and prioritizing threats to IoT systems. It involves understanding both the technical and operational aspects of potential attacks.

Understanding and mitigating IoT risks requires a systematic approach to identifying, evaluating, and reducing vulnerabilities. Risk assessment in IoT environments involves mapping the attack surface, evaluating potential impacts, and implementing proportional defenses.

IoT Attack Surface Mapping

An IoT attack surface includes all possible points where an unauthorized user could interact with or compromise a system. This encompasses devices, communication channels, applications, APIs, and cloud services. Comprehensive mapping helps identify weak spots such as open ports, insecure protocols, and third-party integrations. Visualization tools and automated scanners can assist in maintaining a dynamic understanding of evolving attack surfaces.

Vulnerability Scoring and Prioritization

Not all vulnerabilities pose equal risks. Scoring frameworks such as
the Common Vulnerability Scoring System (CVSS) help organizations
prioritize which issues to address first. In IoT, additional factors such as
device criticality, physical exposure, and potential human safety impact
must also be considered. Automated vulnerability management systems
can streamline patch deployment and configuration hardening across
diverse device fleets.

Threat Modeling Techniques

Threat modeling provides a structured way to anticipate attacker behavior.
Frameworks like STRIDE (Spoofing, Tampering, Repudiation, Information
Disclosure, Denial of Service, Elevation of Privilege) and attack trees
help visualize how IoT components can be compromised. Regular threat
modeling exercises foster proactive defense, aligning security investments
with real-world risks.

Building Resilient IoT Ecosystems

Resilience in IoT systems goes beyond prevention; it emphasizes
detection, response, and recovery. Strategies include adopting zero-
trust architectures, employing hardware root-of-trust mechanisms, and
enforcing secure boot processes. Equally important is collaboration
between manufacturers, service providers, and users to maintain long-
term device security through updates, monitoring, and incident reporting.

Summary

The expansion of the Internet of Things has introduced unprecedented opportunities but also complex cybersecurity challenges.

As IoT technologies evolve, so do the sophistication and diversity of attack vectors.

The proliferation of IoT devices has redefined the boundaries of cybersecurity. From consumer gadgets to national infrastructure, interconnected systems present an ever-expanding attack surface that adversaries continuously exploit. Threat actors—whether hackers seeking profit, nation-states pursuing dominance, or insiders acting carelessly—have demonstrated that IoT vulnerabilities can translate directly into physical and societal consequences.

The case studies and threat analyses presented in this chapter reveal a common truth: the weakest link in IoT security often lies not in technology but in human and organizational behavior. As IoT adoption accelerates, the importance of security-by-design principles, continuous risk assessment, and collaborative defense cannot be overstated. Future threats, driven by AI, quantum computing, and complex supply chains, will only increase in sophistication.

To safeguard the connected world, IoT stakeholders must move beyond reactive defenses and embrace a holistic, adaptive approach to cybersecurity—one that anticipates, withstands, and evolves with the changing threat landscape.

This chapter explored in details the landscape of threats and attack vectors in the IoT ecosystem. It examines the profiles and motives of threat actors, details common and emerging attack methods, analyzes real-world incident case studies, and discusses strategies for risk assessment and attack surface reduction.

We elaborated how threats and cybersecurity attack vectors for IoT encompass a range of vulnerabilities that can be exploited by malicious actors. IoT devices often have weak security standards, such as default or easily guessable passwords, insufficient encryption, and outdated firmware, making them prime targets.

We also discussed about common attack vectors including phishing campaigns that trick users into revealing credentials, malware infections that compromise device functionality, man-in-the-middle attacks intercepting sensitive data, and distributed denial-of-service (DDoS) attacks overwhelming network resources.

We discussed about how threat actors ranging from hackers to nation-states exploit weaknesses in IoT architectures to steal data, disrupt operations, or cause physical harm.

We finally addressed how IoT risks requires a comprehensive approach encompassing risk assessment, secure design principles, continuous monitoring, and international cooperation. Ultimately, building trust in IoT depends on our collective ability to anticipate, defend, and adapt to the ever-changing threat landscape.

CHAPTER 4

Securing the Future of IoT

The Internet of Things (IoT) has emerged as one of the most transformative technological phenomena of the 21st century. Connecting billions of devices—from smartphones and wearables to industrial sensors, autonomous vehicles, smart cities, healthcare equipment, and home appliances—IoT is revolutionizing the way we live, work, and interact with the environment around us. It promises unprecedented levels of convenience, efficiency, and insight, enabling smarter decision-making and fostering innovation across virtually every industry sector.

However, as IoT proliferates, it also exposes new vulnerabilities, creating a complex landscape of security challenges that threaten the integrity, privacy, and resilience of interconnected systems. Unlike traditional IT infrastructure, many IoT devices are resource-constrained, deployed in physically unprotected environments, and often operate with minimal security measures, making them prime targets for cybercriminals and malicious actors.

The rapid expansion of IoT has brought to light critical concerns regarding data privacy, device authenticity, supply chain integrity, and network security. High-profile incidents have demonstrated how compromised IoT devices can be harnessed in large-scale botnets, leading to massive distributed denial-of-service (DDoS) attacks that disrupt

© Massimo Nardone 2026
M. Nardone, *Securing Smart Things*, Apress Pocket Guides,
https://doi.org/10.1007/979-8-8688-2367-1_4

essential services and infrastructure. Moreover, the interconnected nature of IoT means that vulnerabilities in one device or system can cascade, causing widespread damage beyond initial compromise.

In this context, the importance of securing the IoT ecosystem cannot be overstated. It requires a comprehensive, forward-looking approach that integrates technological innovation, rigorous security practices, regulatory compliance, and stakeholder collaboration. As we stand on the cusp of a new era shaped by emerging technologies like 5G, edge computing, and artificial intelligence (AI), the challenge is not only to address existing vulnerabilities but also to anticipate future threats.

"Securing the future of IoT" aims to serve as an authoritative guide and strategic blueprint for organizations, policymakers, researchers, and security practitioners committed to building resilient, trustworthy, and secure IoT environments. The book navigates the complex terrain of IoT security, offering insights into current best practices, innovative approaches, and emerging trends that will shape the security landscape in the years to come.

Throughout this book, we explore key elements that underpin IoT security—from device design and network protection to supply chain integrity and regulatory compliance. We delve into innovative concepts like security-by-design, zero trust architectures, and AI-driven threat detection, emphasizing how these approaches can be effectively implemented to safeguard IoT ecosystems.

This discussion also considers the evolving technological landscape. With the advent of 5G networks, edge computing, and decentralized architectures, the attack surface expands, but so do opportunities for novel security solutions. We examine how these emerging technologies can be harnessed to enhance security, improve resilience, and foster trustworthiness.

Furthermore, our focus extends beyond technology to encompass policy, regulation, and the importance of collaborative efforts across industries and borders. Standards such as GDPR, NIST guidelines, and ISO/IEC 27001 play a crucial role in framing security best practices and ensuring accountability.

This final chapter will outline the essential best practices for IoT security, including securing devices, protecting networks, securing the supply chain, and strengthening data privacy and compliance.

We will introduce the security-by-design principles and the secure development life cycle, explain the roles of network segmentation and monitoring techniques, and discuss about the future role of AI and ML in IoT threat detection.

Finally, we will review regulatory frameworks and compliance standards such as GDPR, NIST, and ISO/IEC 27001 and conclude the book with future trends in IoT security, including 5G, edge computing, and zero trust architecture.

The chapter will discuss about the following:

- **Holistic Approach:** Security must encompass device integrity, network architecture, data privacy, supply chain security, and compliance.

- **Adaptive Technologies:** Leveraging AI, ML, blockchain, and zero trust architectures will be vital in detecting threats early, responding rapidly, and maintaining resilience.

- **Stakeholder Collaboration:** Manufacturers, service providers, policymakers, and end users all play essential roles in establishing a secure IoT ecosystem.

- **Regulatory Alignment:** Staying ahead of standards like GDPR, NIST guidelines, and ISO/IEC 27001 enhances compliance and demonstrates responsibility.

- **Embrace Innovation:** Incorporate emerging technologies thoughtfully, balancing security benefits with operational practicality and resource constraints.

Introduction

As we stated in the previous chapters, the **Internet of Things (IoT)** represents a vast, interconnected ecosystem of physical devices—from industrial robots and medical implants to smart thermostats and connected vehicles—that communicate over digital networks. Unlike traditional computing systems, IoT extends digital connectivity into the physical world, enabling sensors, controllers, and everyday objects to gather, process, and exchange data autonomously.

At its core, IoT is built upon three fundamental layers:

1. **Device Layer:** Sensors and actuators that capture data and interact with the environment

2. **Network Layer:** Communication infrastructure enabling data transmission across wired and wireless mediums

3. **Application Layer:** Platforms and services that process, analyze, and act on device data

The fusion of these layers has revolutionized industries. Manufacturing lines are now predictive rather than reactive, cities are instrumented for energy optimization, and hospitals rely on continuous patient monitoring through wearable devices. Yet, this pervasive connectivity also introduces a radically expanded **attack surface**. Every endpoint becomes a potential doorway for intrusion, exploitation, or data theft.

The Explosion of Connectivity

According to industry estimates, the global IoT ecosystem surpassed **20 billion devices** in deployment by the mid-2020s, with projections exceeding **75 billion by 2030**. This exponential growth is driven by the decreasing cost of sensors, widespread wireless coverage (5G and LPWAN), and increasing reliance on automation and analytics.

However, this expansion often outpaces the maturity of security practices. Many devices are designed for minimal power consumption and low cost, leaving little computational margin for cryptographic functions, secure updates, or strong authentication. The resulting landscape is a paradox—unprecedented innovation paired with fragile defenses.

The interconnectivity among IoT systems also amplifies risk. A single compromised node can propagate malicious traffic, disrupt operations, or be harnessed as part of a **botnet**. The infamous **Mirai botnet** in 2016 exploited thousands of insecure IoT cameras and routers, triggering massive distributed denial-of-service (DDoS) attacks that crippled global websites. Such incidents highlight a grim reality: the weakest device in the network can endanger the entire digital ecosystem.

Why IoT Security Matters

The stakes of IoT insecurity extend far beyond data breaches. Compromised devices can affect **human safety**, **critical infrastructure**, and **national security**. Consider connected medical devices—a vulnerable insulin pump or pacemaker could be life-threatening if remotely tampered with. Industrial control systems (ICS) in energy plants or water treatment facilities face similar perils, as demonstrated by the **Stuxnet** worm that sabotaged nuclear centrifuges via networked controllers.

Furthermore, IoT devices generate massive amounts of **personal and operational data**, often without transparent consent or adequate encryption. When exploited, such data can enable profiling, location tracking, or corporate espionage. The **privacy implications** are profound: IoT blurs the line between the digital and physical realms, where a cyberattack can lead to tangible real-world consequences.

From a business perspective, security failures translate into financial loss, brand erosion, and regulatory penalties. As compliance frameworks like **GDPR** and **NIST IoT guidelines** gain traction, organizations face not only reputational but also legal accountability for inadequate protections.

The Expanding Threat Surface

IoT systems are inherently distributed and heterogeneous. Devices often run on custom operating systems, use proprietary protocols, and interact across multiple administrative domains. This diversity complicates patching, monitoring, and standardization efforts. Many legacy devices were never designed for remote updates, leaving known vulnerabilities permanently exposed.

Typical vulnerabilities include

- **Weak or hardcoded credentials** (e.g., admin/admin logins)

- **Insecure communication channels** lacking encryption

- **Unverified firmware updates** allowing malicious code injection

- **Unpatched third-party libraries** in firmware images

- **Overly permissive APIs** and cloud misconfigurations

Attackers exploit these weaknesses to gain persistence, escalate privileges, or pivot laterally across networks. Once an attacker infiltrates a device, it can serve as a launchpad for more sophisticated intrusions into back-end systems, where sensitive analytics and user data reside.

In short, the IoT environment transforms what used to be isolated computing risks into **systemic, cascading security challenges**.

Balancing Innovation and Risk

The promise of IoT lies in its ability to create smarter, more responsive systems—from precision agriculture and logistics to energy optimization. But innovation must coexist with **responsible security engineering**. Too often, product development prioritizes time-to-market and functionality over resilience. Security is added reactively, if at all.

Adopting a **security-by-design** approach is essential. This means integrating protection mechanisms throughout the entire development life cycle—from architecture and component selection to deployment and maintenance. It requires shifting the mindset from **"add security later"** to **"build securely from the start."**

Moreover, IoT security is not merely a technical problem. It is an **organizational and ecosystem challenge**, involving manufacturers, integrators, network providers, and end users. Effective defense demands collaboration, transparency, and continuous adaptation.

The Economic and Societal Impact

The cost of IoT-related cyber incidents is mounting. Research indicates that global damages from IoT security breaches could exceed **$400 billion annually by 2030**, factoring in operational downtime, data loss, and recovery expenses. Beyond monetary loss, the societal dimension is equally significant: connected systems now underpin essential services—healthcare, transportation, energy, and defense.

An outage in a connected grid or traffic control system could lead to cascading failures across sectors. As the boundary between digital and physical systems dissolves, cybersecurity becomes synonymous with **public safety** and **economic stability**.

Governments and regulatory bodies are beginning to recognize this dependency. Initiatives such as the **US IoT Cybersecurity Improvement Act** and the **EU Cyber Resilience Act** aim to enforce minimum security baselines for manufacturers and service providers. The shift toward legislative enforcement reflects a broader realization: voluntary compliance is no longer sufficient in a hyperconnected world.

Building a Foundation for Trust

Trust is the cornerstone of the IoT economy. Without confidence in device integrity and data authenticity, adoption stalls. Users, whether individuals or enterprises, must believe that connected systems will not compromise their privacy or safety.

Establishing trust in IoT involves several layers:

- **Device Trustworthiness:** Secure boot, verified firmware, and tamper detection

- **Network Trust:** Encrypted communication and authenticated endpoints

- **Data Trust:** Integrity checks, auditability, and provenance tracking

Emerging solutions such as **hardware-based attestation** and **blockchain identity management** are being explored to anchor trust in decentralized environments. However, achieving universal trust requires interoperability—a consistent set of standards and best practices across vendors and industries.

Security As a Continuous Process

Unlike static systems, IoT networks are dynamic—devices join, update, and retire constantly. Therefore, security cannot be a one-time configuration but a **continuous life cycle process**. This involves

- **Ongoing monitoring** for anomalies and threats

- **Timely patching** and over-the-air (OTA) updates

- **Life cycle management** for decommissioning end-of-life devices securely

Organizations must evolve from reactive incident response to proactive **threat anticipation**. Integration of **AI-driven analytics** and **machine learning (ML)** for behavioral detection plays a key role in this evolution.

Toward a Secure and Sustainable IoT Future

As IoT ecosystems expand into every aspect of modern life—from smart homes to autonomous logistics—the imperative for robust security grows exponentially. The challenge lies not only in defending devices but in securing the **entire digital continuum**—spanning hardware, software, networks, and human behavior.

The journey begins with awareness—understanding that every connected object introduces both opportunity and risk. To secure the future of IoT, we must redefine how security is perceived: not as a barrier to innovation, but as its **foundation**.

Privacy-by-Design

Beyond security, IoT systems must respect privacy principles. **Privacy-by-design** extends security-by-design to protect user data integrity and consent:

- Collect only the minimum data required for function

- Use anonymization or pseudonymization where possible

- Implement local processing ("edge privacy") to reduce cloud exposure

- Offer transparency and user control over data collection

- Comply with regulations like **GDPR** and **CCPA** from the design stage

For example, a smart camera should process facial recognition locally, transmitting only metadata, not raw images, to the cloud.

Culture determines success. Organizations that succeed in security-by-design share traits:

- Executive-level ownership of product security

- Dedicated security champions within development teams

- Clear policies for secure coding, testing, and release management

- Measurable KPIs (e.g., vulnerability density, patch response time)

Cross-functional collaboration between engineers, QA, IT, and compliance ensures security decisions are informed, not isolated.

A major smart-meter manufacturer once faced recurring firmware exploits leading to remote tampering. After adopting SDL and secure boot:

- Each firmware release was digitally signed and verified at startup.

- Updates used encrypted OTA delivery with certificate pinning.

- Device telemetry was anonymized before transmission.

- Incident rates dropped by 90%, and compliance with ISO/IEC 27001 was achieved within a year.

The case underscores that **structured process beats reactive patching**. Preventive design yields exponential returns in reliability and trust.

Data Privacy and Protection in IoT

Introduction: Data As the Lifeblood—and Liability—of IoT

In the Internet of Things, data is both the fuel and the footprint. Every connected device continuously generates information—temperature readings, GPS coordinates, heart rate, operational logs—and transmits it to the cloud or to other systems for analysis.

This deluge of telemetry creates immense value. Predictive maintenance saves billions in industrial downtime. Smart cities optimize energy use. Healthcare wearables enable continuous monitoring. Yet, with every byte collected, the boundary between utility and surveillance blurs.

When data becomes the product, **privacy becomes the casualty**. Protecting IoT data is not simply a compliance requirement; it's a moral and operational imperative.

Securing IoT data begins with understanding its journey:

1. **Collection:** Sensors and devices capture raw data, often at high frequency.

2. **Transmission:** Data moves over local networks, gateways, or cellular links.

3. **Processing:** Cloud or edge systems analyze and enrich the data.

4. **Storage:** Information is archived for historical analytics or compliance.

5. **Sharing:** Data may be exchanged with third parties or applications.

6. **Deletion:** At end of life, data must be securely destroyed.

Each stage introduces unique risks—interception, tampering, unauthorized access, or retention beyond necessity.

Unlike traditional IT systems, IoT devices often

- Operate in personal spaces (homes, vehicles, hospitals)

- Collect continuous and granular data, including behavioral patterns

- Lack user interfaces to manage consent or settings

A smart thermostat, for instance, can infer occupancy patterns and daily routines—sensitive information for burglars or advertisers.

Moreover, users seldom know what data is collected, where it's stored, or who accesses it.

The key privacy challenges are therefore **transparency, control, and minimization**.

Privacy-by-Design

To address these challenges, the principle of **privacy-by-design** must be embedded throughout the IoT life cycle—not retrofitted after deployment.

Core principles include

1. **Proactive Not Reactive:** Anticipate and prevent privacy violations before they occur.

2. **Privacy As the Default Setting:** Systems collect the minimum data required, without user action.

3. **Privacy Embedded into Design:** Security and privacy controls are integral, not optional.

4. **End-to-End Security:** Protection extends across data collection, transfer, and deletion.

5. **Transparency:** Clear communication of data handling practices.

6. **User-Centric Control:** Users can view, export, and delete their data easily.

In practice, this may mean designing local data processing (edge AI) to reduce cloud exposure or anonymizing identifiers at collection.

Data Protection Techniques

Several technical mechanisms safeguard IoT data confidentiality and integrity.

Encryption

- **At Rest:** Use AES-256 encryption for device storage, gateways, and databases

- **In Transit:** Implement TLS 1.3 or DTLS for communication channels

- **End-to-End Encryption (E2EE):** Ensures data remains protected from origin to destination, even across intermediaries

- **Key Management:** Employ Hardware Security Modules (HSMs) or Trusted Platform Modules (TPMs) for secure key storage and rotation

Anonymization and Pseudonymization

- Replace personal identifiers with pseudonyms or irreversible hashes

- Aggregate data where possible to reduce identifiability

- Use differential privacy to allow analytics without exposing individual records

Access Control

- Enforce least privilege through role-based access (RBAC) or attribute-based access (ABAC)

- Employ multifactor authentication for all administrative functions

- Implement token-based API access (OAuth 2.0)

Integrity Verification

- Apply checksums and cryptographic hashes to ensure data is not modified in transit or at rest

- Use secure audit trails for traceability

Regulatory and Compliance Frameworks for IoT Security

Regulatory Compliance

IoT developers must navigate a complex regulatory landscape. The three most influential frameworks are the following.

GDPR (General Data Protection Regulation—EU)

- Core principles: lawfulness, fairness, transparency, purpose limitation, data minimization, and accountability.

- Requires **explicit consent** for data collection and **the right to be forgotten**.

- Data controllers must perform **Data Protection Impact Assessments (DPIAs)** for high-risk processing.

CCPA (California Consumer Privacy Act—United States)

- Grants rights to know what data is collected and to opt out of its sale

- Applies to IoT manufacturers offering products or services to California residents

PIPEDA (Canada) and Other Regional Laws

- Emphasize informed consent, access rights, and cross-border data transfer restrictions

For industrial IoT, **NISTIR 8228** provides additional guidance on managing privacy risks.

Introduction: Security As a Shared Legal Obligation

IoT security is no longer a matter of best effort; it is increasingly mandated by law.

As connected devices penetrate critical sectors—healthcare, transport, energy, and consumer electronics—regulators have realized that weak security is a **public safety issue**. The result is a growing ecosystem of laws, frameworks, and certification schemes designed to standardize protection and accountability.

For engineers and organizations, understanding these frameworks is crucial. Compliance is not simply a checkbox exercise—it defines **how** security must be designed, implemented, and maintained throughout the product life cycle.

Why Regulation Matters?

The IoT ecosystem spans thousands of vendors, each with different security maturity levels. Without regulation:

- Devices may ship with default passwords.

- Manufacturers might not provide updates.

- Personal data could be collected and sold without consent.

Regulatory frameworks create **a baseline of responsibility**, ensuring that manufacturers, service providers, and operators uphold minimum security and privacy standards.

Equally, compliance builds **consumer trust** and market access. Devices certified under recognized standards signal reliability—an essential differentiator in increasingly security-conscious markets.

The Global Patchwork of IoT Regulations

IoT regulations are emerging across the world, reflecting local priorities but converging around common principles—secure design, transparency, and accountability—summarized as follows.

European Union: GDPR, CRA, and ETSI EN 303 645

- **GDPR (General Data Protection Regulation):** Governs personal data privacy; requires explicit consent, data minimization, and breach notification.

- **Cyber Resilience Act (CRA):** Enforces cybersecurity-by-design for digital products, including IoT. Manufacturers must provide updates and disclose vulnerabilities.

- **ETSI EN 303 645:** Defines baseline requirements for consumer IoT, such as

  - Unique passwords per device

  - Secure update mechanisms

  - Data deletion and protection

  - Transparent privacy policies

United States: NIST Frameworks and Federal Acts

- **NIST IoT Cybersecurity Framework (NISTIR 8259 series)**

  - Identifies core capabilities: device identification, configuration, data protection, logical access, software update, and cybersecurity state awareness

  - Encourages manufacturers to integrate these from design

- **IoT Cybersecurity Improvement Act (2020)**

  - Requires federal agencies to procure only IoT devices meeting NIST guidelines

  - Introduces vulnerability disclosure and patch management mandates

United Kingdom: PSTI Act (2023)

- The **Product Security and Telecommunications Infrastructure Act** mandates

  - No default passwords

  - Clear vulnerability disclosure contact points

  - Defined minimum support periods for updates

Asia-Pacific Initiatives

- **Japan's Basic Act on Cybersecurity** promotes coordination across ministries for critical IoT infrastructure.

- **Singapore's Cybersecurity Labelling Scheme (CLS):** Provides star-rated labels for consumer IoT devices based on security maturity.

- **Australia's Code of Practice:** Voluntary, aligning with ETSI EN 303 645.

Foundational Frameworks: NIST, ISO, and IEC

Technical and management standards complement legal requirements, offering structured ways to achieve compliance.

NIST Cybersecurity Framework (CSF)

It defines five continuous functions:

1. **Identify:** Assets, risks, and governance

2. **Protect:** Safeguards for critical services

3. **Detect:** Anomalies and events

4. **Respond:** Incident containment

5. **Recover:** Resilience and restoration

For IoT, these translate into discovering connected assets, segmenting networks, monitoring telemetry, and automating remediation.

ISO/IEC 27001—Information Security Management Systems (ISMS)

- Establishes a risk-based management process for information security.

- Requires documented controls, audits, and continuous improvement.

- For IoT organizations, ISO 27001 certification demonstrates operational discipline—from data centers to product development.

ISO/IEC 27701—Privacy Information Management

It extends ISO 27001 for privacy management, aligning with GDPR principles.

It formalizes consent, data handling, and disclosure processes—crucial for IoT environments processing personal information.

IEC 62443—Industrial Automation and Control Systems

- Defines cybersecurity for operational technology (OT) and industrial IoT

- Addresses both technical and process aspects:

  - Secure development life cycle (IEC 62443-4-1)

  - Security levels for control systems (IEC 62443-3-3)

  - Supplier and asset-owner obligations

- Essential for manufacturing, energy, and utilities sectors

Certification and Labeling Programs

Certification transforms compliance into measurable assurance. It enables consumers and enterprises to differentiate trustworthy devices from risky ones.

Examples include

- **UL 2900 Series:** Evaluates software vulnerabilities, access control, and data protection for IoT products.

- **Common Criteria (ISO/IEC 15408):** Offers assurance levels (EAL1–EAL7) for product security evaluation.

- **Cybersecurity Labelling Schemes (CLS)**

  - Singapore's four-level system and similar EU initiatives provide visible trust indicators.

- **CSA STAR and FedRAMP:** For cloud components supporting IoT services.

Certification processes typically involve third-party audits, penetration testing, and documentation reviews.

Auditing and Continuous Compliance

Compliance is a living state. To sustain it:

- **Automate Evidence Collection:** Integrate compliance checks into CI/CD pipelines

- **Policy-as-Code:** Encode security baselines (e.g., CIS Benchmarks) directly into infrastructure definitions

- **Regular Audits:** Combine internal and external reviews

- **Vulnerability Disclosure Programs:** Show proactive risk management

Organizations increasingly adopt **Continuous Compliance Monitoring (CCM)** platforms to map real-time device posture against regulatory requirements.

The Role of AI and Machine Learning in IoT Security

Introduction: Intelligence Meets Scale

The Internet of Things is generating a data deluge no human team can monitor manually. Each device produces telemetry—connection logs, sensor outputs, configuration changes—that together create billions of signals per minute. Traditional rule-based defenses can't keep up with that volume or with attackers who mutate their tactics daily.

Enter **artificial intelligence (AI)** and **machine learning (ML)**. AI provides adaptive, data-driven defense: systems that learn from patterns, detect anomalies, and even predict threats before they materialize. In IoT, where endpoints are resource-constrained and distributed, ML offers both **speed** and **autonomy**.

Why Is AI Essential for IoT Security?

1. **Scale:** Millions of heterogeneous devices, each with unique behavior profiles.

2. **Velocity:** Events occur in real time; latency in detection equals exposure.

3. **Variety:** Logs, packet data, firmware metrics, environmental context—high-dimensional inputs.

4. **Evasion:** Attackers use automation and AI themselves; static defenses must evolve dynamically.

AI shifts security from reactive signatures to **behavioral understanding**—learning what "normal" looks like and flagging deviations instantly.

Table 4-1 shows the machine learning techniques in IoT security.

Table 4-1. *Machine Learning Techniques in IoT Security*

Technique	Use case	Example
Supervised learning	Classify benign vs. malicious traffic	Random forest model trained on labeled network flows
Unsupervised learning	Detect unknown anomalies	Autoencoders or clustering on sensor telemetry
Reinforcement learning	Optimize adaptive firewall policies	Agent adjusts thresholds to minimize false alarms
Deep learning	Recognize complex multistage attacks	CNN/LSTM analyzing temporal-spatial patterns
Federated learning	Collaborative defense without sharing raw data	Edge devices train local models and share gradients

These methods form the backbone of intelligent intrusion detection and self-healing networks.

AI-Driven Anomaly Detection

In traditional security, thresholds are static: "Alert if CPU > 90 %." AI replaces those heuristics with **contextual baselines**—learning per-device behavior, time of day, and operational state.

Example:

A water-pump sensor typically sends 60 packets/hour. When an attacker hijacks it for scanning, the traffic jumps to 10,000 packets/hour.

An ML model flags this anomaly instantly, triggering quarantine before damage spreads.

Edge-deployed inference models make this possible with millisecond latency and minimal bandwidth.

Predictive Threat Intelligence

AI doesn't just detect—it forecasts.

By analyzing global telemetry, threat feeds, and exploit trends, models can predict

- Emerging attack vectors targeting specific firmware versions

- Geographical propagation of new botnets

- Correlations between vulnerability disclosures and scanning spikes

Predictive analytics enable **proactive patching** and **risk prioritization**, moving organizations from firefighting to foresight.

Ethical and Legal Considerations

- **Bias:** Training data skew can misclassify legitimate device behavior.

- **Accountability:** Who is liable for an automated defensive action that halts production?

- **Privacy:** Continuous monitoring may conflict with data protection laws.

- **Transparency:** Regulations increasingly demand explainable AI decisions.

Security automation must include human oversight loops and auditable logs to remain compliant and ethical.

Future of AI in IoT Security

Expect AI to evolve toward

- **Cognitive SOCs:** Security operations centers fully augmented by ML

- **Cross-Domain Learning:** Sharing patterns between IT, OT, and IoT contexts

- **Quantum-Resistant ML:** Integrating postquantum cryptography for secure model exchange

- **Autonomous Agents:** Self-defending devices negotiating trust dynamically

Emerging Technologies and Their Security Implications

Technological revolutions never arrive alone. 5G, edge computing, blockchain, and quantum advances are reshaping how devices connect and trust each other. While these innovations boost performance and flexibility, they also **redraw the threat surface**. Understanding their security implications is key to preparing for the next wave of IoT.

5G: The New Nervous System of IoT

Opportunities:

- Massive device density (up to 1 million devices/km^2)

- Ultra-low latency (< 1 ms)

- Network slicing for customized QoS

Risks:

- Expanded attack surface across virtualized network functions (NFV)

- Misconfigured slices leading to cross-tenant data leaks

- Supply chain exposure through third-party 5G components

Mitigation: Adopt **zero trust 5G architectures**, secure APIs, and continuous monitoring of virtualized network elements.

Edge and Fog Computing

Processing data closer to its source reduces latency and bandwidth but disperses the attack perimeter.

Security imperatives include

- Mutual authentication between edge nodes and cloud

- Encrypted container images and signed workloads

- Runtime attestation to ensure node integrity

- Localized AI for threat detection

Standardization efforts like **OpenFog Security Framework** guide design for trustworthy distributed edge platforms.

Zero Trust Architecture (ZTA)

ZTA replaces perimeter defense with continuous verification.

Principles:

- Assume breach—verify every request

- Authenticate identity, device health, and context

- Enforce least privilege dynamically

In IoT, ZTA means microsegmentation at the device level, just-in-time credentials, and policy engines evaluating real-time telemetry before granting access.

Blockchain and Distributed Ledger Technologies

DLT introduces decentralized trust—ideal for verifying IoT transactions without central authorities.

Use cases:

- **Identity Management:** Immutable device credentials

- **Supply Chain Tracking:** Provenance for components and updates (see Chapter 5)

- **Secure Data Sharing:** Smart contracts controlling access

Challenges: Scalability, energy consumption, and privacy of on-chain data. Hybrid approaches (off-chain storage + on-chain verification) mitigate these.

Quantum Computing and Postquantum Cryptography

Quantum computers threaten classical encryption by solving factoring problems exponentially faster.

For IoT, migration must start early:

- Evaluate dependence on RSA/ECC keys

- Adopt **postquantum algorithms** (CRYSTALS-Kyber, Dilithium)

- Implement crypto-agility—ability to upgrade algorithms without hardware change

NIST's ongoing PQC standardization will define future-proof baselines.

Digital Twins and Cyber-Physical Simulation

Digital twins mirror real-world assets in software for predictive analysis.

Security implications:

- Unauthorized access could manipulate physical operations.

- Integrity of twin-to-device synchronization is critical.

- Data consistency and version control prevent sabotage.

Applying encryption, identity federation, and audit trails ensures safe simulation-to-reality feedback loops.

Self-Healing and Autonomous Systems

Next-gen IoT devices will self-diagnose and repair using AI orchestration:

- Detect configuration drift

- Restore firmware autonomously

- Negotiate secure reenrollment if compromised

These systems blur the line between cybersecurity and cyber-resilience, emphasizing survivability over perfection.

Convergence of IT, OT, and IoT

As industrial systems integrate with enterprise IT, once-isolated networks merge.

Security strategy must bridge different cultures and life cycles: IT's rapid patching vs. OT's uptime obsession.

Unified visibility, shared threat intelligence, and governance frameworks (IEC 62443 + ISO 27001) are essential.

Future Trends and Strategic Outlook

IoT is entering its maturity phase. The coming decade will be defined less by expansion and more by **stabilization, governance, and intelligence**.

Security will shift from static defense to adaptive ecosystems capable of learning, negotiating, and evolving autonomously.

Trend 1: Security as a Service (SecaaS) for IoT

Cloud providers will offer managed security stacks—device attestation, threat analytics, and patch orchestration—as subscription services.

Small manufacturers will rely on these shared infrastructures, democratizing advanced protection once available only to large enterprises.

Trend 2: Regulatory Convergence and Global Baselines

Expect consolidation around ISO 27001 + ETSI EN 303 645 + NIST 8259 as a de facto global baseline.

Mutual recognition among jurisdictions will simplify certification, enabling "security passports" for devices crossing borders.

Trend 3: Autonomous, Self-Defending Ecosystems

Building on AI progress, IoT networks will become **self-managing organisms**:

- Continuous risk scoring per device

- Automated microsegmentation and patching

- Cooperative defense swarms sharing threat intelligence peer to peer

This evolution echoes biological immune systems—distributed, adaptive, and resilient.

Trend 4: Privacy-Enhancing Computation

Federated analytics, homomorphic encryption, and confidential computing will allow organizations to collaborate on shared datasets without revealing raw information—solving the long-standing conflict between innovation and privacy.

Trend 5: Energy-Aware and Sustainable Security

IoT's carbon footprint is under scrutiny.

Future security algorithms will prioritize **energy efficiency**: lightweight cryptography, duty-cycled sensors, and adaptive encryption levels balancing risk and power consumption.

Trend 6: Human-Machine Collaboration

Even in automated environments, human judgment remains central.

Security operations will evolve into **Human-in-the-Loop AI** models—AI handles scale, while humans handle ethics, context, and accountability.

As a conclusion from protection to resilience, the goal of IoT security is no longer to build impregnable walls—it is to create **resilient ecosystems** capable of absorbing shocks, adapting, and recovering.

Security-by-design, powered by AI, anchored in compliance, and guided by ethics, forms the blueprint for this resilient future.

The secure IoT of tomorrow will not emerge by chance but by deliberate architecture—**a** partnership between technology, policy, and human responsibility.

Summary

Securing the future of IoT is a complex, ongoing endeavor that demands a multifaceted approach, integrating current best practices, technological innovations, and compliance with emerging standards. The rapid adoption of 5G, proliferation of IoT devices, and adoption of edge and decentralized architectures all present opportunities and vulnerabilities that require vigilant, adaptive security strategies.

Fundamentally, organizations must embrace proactive security measures from the outset—incorporating security-by-design principles and embedding continuous monitoring and threat intelligence into their operations. This approach not only mitigates risks but also builds trust with consumers, partners, and regulators.

By adopting these strategies, organizations can not only protect their IoT systems from current threats but also future-proof their infrastructures against evolving cyber threats. Investing in ongoing research, workforce training, and cross-sector collaboration will ensure that IoT remains a transformative force—delivering benefits securely, ethically, and sustainably.

As IoT continues to integrate deeper into our daily lives and critical infrastructure, security becomes more than a technical necessity—it becomes a fundamental enabler of trust, innovation, and societal progress. The path forward requires vigilance, agility, and a shared commitment to cultivating a resilient, secure IoT environment that can withstand the challenges of tomorrow.

This chapter explored in detail the essential best practices for IoT security, including securing devices, protecting networks, securing the supply chain, and strengthening data privacy and compliance.

We introduced the security-by-design principles and the secure development life cycle, explained the roles of network segmentation and monitoring techniques, and discussed the future role of AI and ML in IoT threat detection.

We also described the most important regulatory frameworks and compliance standards such as GDPR, NIST, and ISO/IEC 27001.

We concluded the book with future trends in IoT security, including 5G, edge computing, and zero trust architecture.